GOD'S STORY

GOD'S STORY

A STUDENT'S GUIDE TO CHURCH HISTORY

BRIAN COSBY

CF4·K

10 9 8 7 6 5 4 3 2 1
© Copyright 2014 Brian Cosby
ISBN: 978-1-78191-320-8

Published in 2014
by
Christian Focus Publications,
Geanies House, Fearn, Tain,
Ross-shire, IV20 1TW, U.K.

Cover design by Paul Lewis
Printed and bound by Bell and Bain, Glasgow

MIX
Paper from
responsible sources
FSC® C007785

CONTENTS

To

J. Ligon Duncan III

for his inspiration to study the past

INTRODUCTION:
WHY STUDY CHURCH HISTORY?

Igrumbled to my mother, "What does Henry VIII have to do with me?" I was seventeen years old and in the middle of a European History class at school. As my *least* favorite subject, history seemed utterly pointless and irrelevant.

Fast-forward three years. Once again, I found myself sitting in a history class, though this time as a freshman at Samford University in Birmingham, Alabama. Samford requires all of its students to take a certain number of basic courses, history included. For whatever reason—I'll credit the professor—the stories of the past came alive and I became more and more enamored with the people, the movements, and the watershed events that transformed culture and civilization. In a few short days, I switched from a course of business to a course of history, eventually graduating with it as my major.

You might be in the same boat asking, "Why study history?" The book you're holding is a brief overview of the history of the Christian church, which leads us to ask, "Why study *church* history?" It's a fair question. Let me give you four reasons why I believe knowing church history is beneficial.

First, *knowing church history helps explain our identity.* Who are the people of God? Where did we come from? Assuming you are a Christian, you have been *re*born into a multi-ethnic worldwide family. Church history points us to the God who chose a people for himself from before the foundation of the world (Eph. 1:4). The church—which is the bride (Rev. 21:9) and body (Eph. 4:12) of Christ—is made up of all those who are called out[1] of the world as God's treasured possession (Deut. 7:6). If you are a Christian, these chosen people (1 Pet. 2:9) are your spiritual family—a long line of sinners and saints.

Second, *knowing church history helps explain the present.* What is the history and heritage of your local church? Is it part of a denomination? Why? Does your church recite the Apostles' Creed or hold to a confession of faith like the *Westminster Confession of Faith*? Knowing the past helps explain the present—what we do, why we

---

[1] The Greek word for "church" in the New Testament is *ekklesia*, which means to be "called out."

baptize infants (or not), and why you have a local church at all! Whether you realize it or not, you are affected by your family's history, your nation's history, and your church's history. Knowing our past helps explain our present.

Third, *knowing church history guards us from repeating its mistakes.* You've probably heard it said, "History repeats itself." This is true! As you will no doubt see throughout the course of this book, church history is replete with controversy, heresy, envy, strife, sin, arrogance, and foolishness. We see how pride has led to ruin, anger to murder, and lust to adultery. We see how errors in understanding the Bible led to unintended consequences and how abandoning the Bible altogether led to a slippery slope of disastrous proportions. There have been countless times that I have been able to recognize a current trend in the church *today*—with its unintended consequences—simply by being familiar with church history. Knowing the past helps guard us from repeating the same errors in the present and future.

Fourth, *knowing church history testifies to God's powerful working as HIS STORY.* Despite the sin and folly of the church, God overrules our sin for his good purposes. Indeed, history is *his story!* It testifies to the

God who will work all things according to the counsel of his will (Eph. 1:11), whatever his hand and plan have predestined to take place (Acts 4:28). He has declared the end from the beginning (Isa. 46:10) and calls us to take part in his tapestry of salvation. The scarlet thread running throughout the pages of history is the God who is, at once, sovereign, good, holy, self-sufficient, eternal, unchangeable, loving, and faithful to his church.

In the pages to follow, I have tried to only address what I see as the poignant people, councils, events, revivals, and movements throughout the history of the church. Thus, in striving for brevity, I have left out many others. It is my hope that this brief primer will serve to whet your appetite for a deeper and more-extensive study of God's story. Indeed, it is God who we are to see and worship—as he has saved, preserved, sustained, and refined a people for his own glory.

THE CHURCH AND ITS OLD TESTAMENT ROOTS

I used to play football (or "soccer" in the US) for my school as a teenager and I still love watching football on television. Few things are more thrilling than when you see a pre-determined plan unfolding before your eyes between members of a team as they move the ball down the field, ending in an exhilarating strike to the back of the net. The fans go wild—chest bumping and cheering—and the players dog-pile on top of each other like a multi-layered human sandwich.

It's what they have practiced over and over again for years. Sometimes, a goal happens as a seemingly unintentional fluke. But those *pre-planned* executions—where everything happens according to what they've practiced—seem to captivate the crowd, building up their excitement until the ball blasts past the goalkeeper and the stadium erupts into all-out elation, or at least half of the stadium.

The history of the church is God's *pre-determined* plan. It's his "Plan A." Despite the sin, corruption, and twisted events in the church's past, God has preserved a remnant, his people. In fact, you are reading this page according to the eternal plan of God!

Even though this book focuses on the history of the church after the days of Jesus to the present times, its origin certainly did not begin there. Before the creation of the heavens and the earth, God chose a people from every tribe and language and people and nation to be his treasured possession (Eph. 1:4; Rev. 5:9). This is the true church of God and it will persevere *as* the church of God into glory.

The Church Visible and Invisible

At the outset, an important distinction needs to be made between the church *invisible* and the church *visible*. No, I'm not talking about ghosts or people walking around who can't be seen. The church *invisible* doesn't mean that you can't see it; rather, it's made up of all those—in every age—who have been saved by God's grace alone through faith alone in Jesus Christ alone. It's the true church, ransomed by the blood of Jesus Christ.

Those who represent the *visible* church, on the other hand, may or may not be a member of God's chosen and saved people. They are members of the local visible church—the people you see in the pews or seats at church, those who make public professions of faith and so on. Jesus said that there exists tares among the wheat (Matt. 13:29-30), goats among the sheep (Matt. 25:32), and unbelievers among believers (cf. 1 John 2:19).

The church invisible exists within and alongside the church visible. At times, as we will see throughout the course of this book, we are astounded by the sheer worldliness and sin of the "church." But we must remember that many who make up the visible church are not true believers. For one reason or another—whether power, prestige, community, emotional support, etc.—they are aligned with the church by profession of faith, but in the end, Jesus will say to them the sobering words, "I never knew you, depart from me, you workers of lawlessness" (Matt. 7:23). To be sure, Jesus alone is the Head of the church (Col. 1:18) and he will build his church and the gates of hell will not prevail against it (Matt. 16:18).

But the good news is that God, by his good and sovereign grace, has saved a rebellious, spiritually dead people through the life, death, and resurrection of his Son, Jesus Christ, whose atoning work on the cross and righteousness is applied to the elect by the working of the Holy Spirit, which we receive by faith alone. The true church consists of all those who have experienced this new birth by trusting in Jesus Christ as Savior and Lord.

The Old Testament Church

We see the beginning of God's people from the beginning of the Old Testament where God promises a coming Messiah. After Adam and Eve's fall into sin, God said, "I will put enmity between you [the serpent] and the woman, and between your offspring and her offspring; he shall bruise your head, and you shall bruise his heel" (Gen. 3:15). From the very beginning, then, we see two offspring, two people: those *of the world*—following Satan—and those *of God*, trusting in him and his saving promises. This difference becomes more and more apparent as you move through the pages of the Bible between Cain and Abel (Gen. 4), between Noah's family and the families of the world (Gen. 6), and between Israel and its surrounding nations.

But the church really began to take shape when God called Abram (later renamed "Abraham") as the father of a new visible community of faith. God told Abram,

Go from your country and your kindred and your father's house to the land that I will show you. I will make of you a great nation, and I will bless you and make your name great, so that you will be a blessing.

*I will bless those who bless you, and him
who dishonors you I will curse, and in you
all the families of the earth shall be blessed
(Gen. 12:1-3).*

Abraham fathered Isaac and Isaac fathered
Jacob. Throughout Israel's history, God
continued to remember his covenant
promises by reminding his people that he
remains the God of "Abraham, Isaac, and
Jacob." Jacob had twelve sons, whose
names represented the twelve tribes of
Israel. God's Old Testament church, Israel,
would eventually make their way to Egypt
under the care of one of Jacob's sons,
Joseph, who became second in command
over all of Egypt.

After 430 years, Israel found herself
in slavery under an Egyptian ruler who
treated them harshly as slaves. So God
called Moses to lead his people out of
slavery—called the *Exodus.* This was the
defining event of deliverance for the Old
Testament church. God's people made
their way through the desert to Mount
Sinai, where God gave Moses and Israel
the Ten Commandments (Exod. 20) and
the Levitical laws. If they kept God's
commands, they would live long in the
land that God was giving to them. If not,
they would be cursed and punished.

At once, they rebelled and refused to go into the Promised Land, Canaan. As a result, a whole generation died in the wilderness (the book of Numbers). Even Moses, because of his sin, would not enter the Promised Land. When they did finally enter Canaan, under the leadership of Joshua, it wasn't long before they rebelled and worshiped the gods of the Canaanites and fell into a cycle of sin and judgment (the book of Judges). Looking to the surrounding nations instead of to their God, they sought to have a human king and found their first king in Saul (1 Sam. 8-9). Saul eventually rejected the Lord through his sin and so God chose a "man after his own heart," David (1 Sam. 13:14).

Despite King David's many infamous sins of murder, adultery, and greed—think of the story of Bathsheba!—his life and monarchy would become a standard for the future kings of Israel. Ultimately, his kingship would point to the truer and greater King, Jesus Christ. Worship in the newly-constructed temple became part and parcel of Israel's worship after David, under the leadership of his son, Solomon. The sacrificial, ceremonial, and moral laws given to Moses at Mount Sinai would remain in place, giving the Old Testament church the basic structure for religious life and worship. These sacrifices and ceremonies, too, would point to the sacrificial Lamb of God, Jesus Christ, who died once and for all his people (Heb. 7:27). Through sin and strife, Israel divided into two kingdoms, "Israel" in the north and "Judah" in the south (1 Kings 12).

Over and over, God sent prophets to his people to warn them of judgment and exile if they did not obey his laws and commandments (2 Chron. 36:15-16). But they continued to rebel against the Lord. Finally, by his sovereign displeasure, he punished his people. The Assyrians conquered the northern kingdom, Israel, in 722 B.C. and the Babylonians conquered the southern kingdom, Judah, in 586 B.C.

But God was gracious and remained faithful to his remnant and—through the Persian King Cyrus—God caused his people to return to their land and rebuild around 538 B.C. (Ezra 1). How did God's people respond? At first, they responded with great thankfulness and praise. But once again, despite the overflowing mercy of God's grace, they gave him half-hearted worship and continued to do what was right in their *own* eyes. They did not worship God as he had instructed them nor did they keep the laws he had commanded.

Hope in the Coming Messiah

But God continued to point his people to the coming Messiah. This Messiah-King would be born of a virgin (Isa. 7:14) from the little town of Bethlehem (Micah 5:2) as a "light for the nations" (Isa. 42:6). He would come "humble and mounted on a donkey" (Zech. 9:9) and would be "wounded for our transgressions" and "crushed for our iniquities" (Isa. 53:5). This Messiah would be the "righteous branch" (Jer. 23:5) and, through him, God would make a "new covenant" with his people, one built upon his own promise and design (Jer. 31:31) rather than the conditional, obedience-based covenant with his people *as a nation* (Exod. 19ff.).

But God also remained faithful to his promise that he gave to Abraham that, through him, all the nations and families of the earth would be blessed. In fact, those who came after Christ, called "Christians," would be referred to as "the sons of Abraham" (Gal. 3:7). God spoke to his people through the prophet Joel and said, "And it shall come to pass afterward, that I will pour out my Spirit on all flesh ... everyone who calls on the name of the LORD shall be saved" (Joel 2:28, 32). God's plan of salvation would go beyond the Jews to include the Gentiles.

For about four hundred years, the Lord remained silent—what we call the inter-testamental period between our Old and New Testaments (600 B.C. to 0). And then, the prophecies and promises began to unfold, as the Ancient of Days became the Infant of Days; God took on flesh as the long-expected Messiah.

This was all God's "Plan A." As the apostle Paul wrote to young Timothy, "[God] saved us and called us to a holy calling, not because of our works but because of his own purpose and grace, *which he gave us in Christ Jesus before the ages began*" (2 Tim. 1:9, emphasis mine). In God's eternal perspective, Jesus is the Lamb slain from "before the foundation of the world" (Rev. 13:8). God had called a people, Israel, and established laws and commandments, all of which pointed to the One who would fulfill them in his life, death, and resurrection. A child was born, but a Son was given (Isa. 9:6). Salvation would come from the Jews (John 4:22) in the person and work of Jesus Christ. The New Testament church had begun.

DISCUSSION QUESTIONS

- If you had to define the "church," what would you say?
- How is the church different and how is it the same between the Old and New Testaments?
- What's the difference between the church visible and the church invisible?
- How can you be in the world, but not of the world?

THE NEW TESTAMENT CHURCH AND APOSTOLIC FATHERS (A.D. 1-100)

For a brief time I lived in London while in college. Until then, I never knew that milk could be purchased in unrefrigerated boxes. The only milk I knew of came in cold plastic jugs. Not that it mattered much, but drinking room-temperature milk out of a box took some getting used to! Of course it's the same kind of milk, just different packaging.

The same kind of reality can be said of an event in the news. One event, like the Golden Jubilee of Elizabeth II in 2012, was reported in hundreds (if not thousands) of newspapers around the world. It's the same event, just different accounts and perspectives.

The four Gospels, located at the beginning of the New Testament—Matthew, Mark, Luke, and John—all present the same story about the same person, just different angles. They are four complimentary real accounts about the life, ministry, death, and resurrection of Jesus Christ. Near the beginning of his public ministry, Jesus called twelve men (the disciples), trained them, and then sent them out as his ministers. No, these were not super-special or particularly holy guys; they were "twelve ordinary men."[1]

At times, these men seemed unshakable and full of faith. At other times, however, they were afraid, unbelieving, and cowardly. They liked basking in the spotlight when Jesus was popular (who doesn't?), but fled and ran away when he was arrested. It was upon the testimony of these ordinary men that Jesus chose to build his church. Indeed, we are but "jars of clay, to show that the surpassing power belongs to God and not to us" (2 Cor. 4:7). The disciples' *message* was the gospel, the "good news" that God has sent his only Son into the world to save sinners and to reconcile a people to himself.

After Easter

Jesus' crucifixion in the year A.D. 33 surprised everybody. The One that a growing number of Jews expected to overthrow the Romans—the people who ruled over the Jews at the time of Jesus—was humiliated and killed like a common criminal! Even though God had foretold the Messiah's death through the Old Testament prophets, the fledgling little church was shocked at the

[1] See John MacArthur, *Twelve Ordinary Men: How the Master Shaped His Disciples for Greatness, and What He Wants to Do With You* (Nashville: Thomas Nelson, 2006).

reality. After Jesus breathed his last, Roman soldiers pierced his side with a spear just to make sure he was dead.

His body was taken down from the cross and laid in the tomb of Joseph of Arimathea, a member of the Jewish council (cf. Luke 23:50-53). But on the third day— Easter Sunday—Jesus rose from the dead, thereby validating his atoning death on the cross. History would never be the same.

Luke, the historian, physician, and travelling companion of the apostle Paul, records a fascinating account of Jesus after his resurrection. Two disciples of Jesus were travelling to a village named Emmaus, reeling from the news that Jesus was crucified. Jesus himself drew near and went with them and asked them about their conversation. At first they didn't recognize him and they didn't understand all that had taken place. Jesus said to them,

O foolish ones, and slow of heart to believe all that the prophets have spoken! Was it not necessary that the Christ should suffer these things and enter into his glory? And beginning with Moses and all the Prophets, he interpreted to them in all the Scriptures the things concerning himself (Luke 24:25-27).

Remember that this is *God's* story, his sovereign plan. He had planned and determined the death of Jesus from before the foundation of the world. Jesus' mission was to redeem his sheep, his bride, his people. He didn't die *in hopes* that people might believe, but rather he died to sovereignly save those who would believe. Make no mistake: Jesus was "delivered up according to the definite plan and foreknowledge of God" (Acts 2:23).

Over and over again—for some forty days after his resurrection—Jesus proved that he was the Christ, the Savior of sinners (cf. Acts 1:3). He appeared to individuals, groups, and skeptics, many of whom were still alive when the New Testament letters were being written (cf. 1 Cor. 15:6)! He ate with them and assured them of his continual presence, even "to the end of the age" (Matt. 28:20).

Acts: The Spread of the Early Church

Before he ascended to the right hand of his Father in heaven, Jesus told his disciples, "You will receive power when the Holy Spirit has come upon you, and you will be my witnesses in Jerusalem and in all Judea and Samaria, and to the end of the earth" (Acts 1:8). This is the guiding pattern throughout the book of Acts; the church would spread from Jerusalem out to the uttermost parts of the earth. But, rather ironically, this would happen *through persecution* and the death of God's people.

The book of Acts in the New Testament is a historical narrative of the events of the early church after the ascension of Jesus into heaven. In particular, it follows the mission and ministry of the apostles *Peter* (chapters 1-12) and *Paul* (chapters 13-28). Peter's ministry centers in Jerusalem while Paul's ministry expands to the Gentiles around the Mediterranean. The early church devoted themselves to the apostles' teaching, fellowship, the sacraments, worship, prayer, and service (Acts 2:42-46). The result? "The Lord added to their number day by day those who were being saved" (v. 47). There was nothing fancy about their ministry—no gimmicks, no light shows, no dueling DJs. They simply sought to be faithful in planting and watering the gospel of Jesus through these basic means.

Miracles, signs, and wonders also accompanied the early spread of the gospel as visible proofs of the new revelation being communicated. The blind could see, the lame walked, and the apostles seemed to possess supernatural authority to cast out demons and heal various individuals. Indeed, new Scripture was being added to the body of Scripture that we call the "Old Testament." This new revelation, given through the apostles, was just as inspired, infallible, and authoritative as the Old and is what we now call the "New Testament." In fact, Peter himself called Paul's writings "scripture" (2 Pet. 3:16)! The healings, signs, and wonders served to validate God's new revelation as seen in the pages of the New Testament.

As mentioned, persecution spurred the spread of the early church. After the stoning of Stephen (an early deacon), Luke writes, "And there arose on that day a great persecution against the church in Jerusalem, and they were all *scattered* throughout the regions of Judea and Samaria" (Acts 8:1, emphasis mine). Notice how this supports Jesus' promise given in Acts 1:8, "You will be my witnesses in Jerusalem and in all Judea and Samaria, and to the end of the earth."

Eventually, both Peter and Paul would be killed as martyrs for their faith in Christ; Peter by crucifixion upside down (he didn't think it proper to be crucified the same way as his Lord) and Paul by beheading, both around A.D. 65 in Rome under the reign of the Emperor Nero.[2] The apostle John would out-survive both of them, living into the 90s, during which time he wrote his Gospel account as well as his epistles and the book of Revelation.

[2] These dates are approximate, as we do not have specific historical record.

The Apostolic Fathers

During the first century, persecution against Christians ebbed and flowed. During the early 80s the Romans really began to target Christians. Under the Roman emperor, Domitian (A.D. 51-96), Christian worship was banned and Jews and Christians both were required to send their tithe money to Rome. Many refused and suffered the consequences. This intentional persecution against Christians strengthened over time and would continue as official Roman practice until the early 300s. Much of the history of the early church is seen against this backdrop of persecution.

A number of men took up the mantle as leaders of the early church during and soon after the apostles died, called "the Apostolic Fathers," a designation that indicates their close connection to the apostles. Particularly, among these were Clement of Rome, Ignatius of Antioch, and Polycarp of Smyrna. These men would help bridge the teachings of the apostles in the first century to many of the early church leaders in the second century. All three would die a martyr's death.

Clement of Rome
Clement, who was a successor of the apostle Peter and called "Bishop" of Rome, was most likely the "Clement" mentioned by the

apostle Paul in Philippians 4:3 as his fellow laborer in the ministry. Ancient sources note that Clement knew the apostle Peter and is, to this day, ascribed by the Roman Catholic Church as the fourth Bishop (or "Pope") of Rome.[3]

Clement governed the church in Rome, where there existed a large number of Christians. After A.D. 64—when the emperor Nero unjustly blamed a massive fire in Rome on the Christians—and especially after Domitian became emperor in A.D. 81, persecution became much more intense. But despite the cruel torture and executions of these early Christians, the church continued to grow and spread. Clement no doubt experienced much of this persecution.

Around A.D. 96, Clement wrote a letter, called *First Clement*,[4] to the Christian church in Corinth (in Greece), in which he affirmed the authority of bishops and presbyters (elders) in the church. As we shall see in the following chapters, this declaration of "authority" would be a key argument of the Church of Rome down through the ages. Clement was eventually banished to the

---

[3] The Bishop of Rome is also the Pope in the Roman Catholic Church.

[4] *Second Clement*, another letter originally ascribed to Clement, was later subject to intense scrutiny after the historian Eusebius (263-339) noted that there existed only *one* letter to this Clement, raising doubts that it really was genuine.

modern-day Crimean peninsula in A.D. 99 to serve hard labor in a stone quarry and, two years later, tied to an anchor and thrown from a boat into the Black Sea.

Ignatius of Antioch
Ignatius (c.35-c.108) presided as an early bishop in the city of Antioch, located on the eastern side of the Mediterranean Sea. Significantly, he was also a disciple of the apostle John. At one point, Roman authorities arrested him and as they brought him to Rome, he wrote a series of letters, which outlined some very important theology. First, Ignatius (rightly) argued that Jesus was both fully divine and fully human. A group of false teachers promoting *Docetism* were insisting that Jesus only *appeared* to be human, but was really only spirit and not flesh. In response, Ignatius insisted that Jesus was not only divine, but also fully man, a topic that the apostle John dealt with in his Gospel account and in his epistles.

Second, Ignatius stressed the need for *unity*, but not just any unity. The unity of Jesus' two natures—divine and human— laid the foundation for the unity of the church. If one denied the unity of Christ's two natures, he or she could also deny the unity of Christ's body, the church.

Third, like many early Christians, Ignatius saw suffering for the sake of Jesus as an aspect of Christian discipleship. Since discipleship meant following in the footsteps of Jesus, this included a life of suffering, which was welcomed by many of the early Christians. To flee persecution and martyrdom (dying for faith in Christ) was the equivalent of denying Jesus himself. In his journey from Antioch to Rome under Roman guard, Ignatius wrote, "Let me be food for the wild beast ... then I will truly be a disciple of Jesus Christ." Indeed, he would be led to the famous Coliseum in Rome where, according to tradition, he was eaten by lions.

Polycarp of Smyrna
Ignatius' friend, Polycarp (c.69-c.155), was also a disciple of the apostle John. He led the church in Smyrna, a city located on the western coast of modern-day Turkey (not too far from Ephesus). During a visit to Rome to discuss the celebration of Easter festivals and calendars, he was arrested. The Romans commanded him to worship the Roman emperor by burning incense. Polycarp refused and, thus, they sentenced him to death.

The account of Polycarp's death is one of the most memorable and remarkable martyrdoms of the early church. When asked why he wouldn't reject his Lord, Jesus,

Polycarp responded: "Eighty and six years I have served him, and he has done me no wrong. How then can I blaspheme my King and Savior? Bring forth what thou wilt." He was tied to a stake and burned.

As far as Polycarp's legacy goes, some sources indicate that it was Polycarp who first compiled the books and letters of the New Testament. In fact, in the only extant letter attributed to him—*Letter to the Philippians*—he relies heavily on the New Testament documents. In this letter, Polycarp exhorts the Philippians to persevere in their Christian witness: "Stand fast, therefore, in this conduct and follow the example of the Lord." Polycarp would prove to be a significant bridge connecting the apostles to later leaders of the church, called the "Church Fathers." His dates overlap the life of his mentor, the apostle John, with later church leaders like Irenaeus (c.130-c.200), Clement of Alexandria (c.150-c.215), and Tertullian (c.160-c.225). This last Church Father, Tertullian, once commented, "The blood of martyrs is the seed of the church." As we have seen, his comment is substantiated by a myriad of faithful believers who have followed in the footsteps of their Savior.

In addition to the leadership and literature of the Apostolic Fathers, we have thousands of manuscripts of the New

Testament in Greek (the original language of the New Testament). Moreover, other first century literature, like the *Didache,* provides detailed description of the teachings of the early Christians. Without a doubt, the foundation of Christianity enjoys widespread manuscript evidence and support. The church established by Jesus, governed by the apostles, and led by the early fathers of the faith, has continued down through the ages. We can rest on the overwhelming testimony of the New Testament historical documents, teaching, and witness to the living God, whose story continues today.

DISCUSSION QUESTIONS

- The disciples seemed to fluctuate between being very bold for their faith and being scared. Do you ever experience these swings in your Christian walk?

- After Jesus was raised from the dead, how did he prove that he was indeed the risen Christ?

- The good news of Jesus spread through persecution of God's people. What kinds of persecution did they face? What happened to Peter and Paul?

- There were a number of heresies in the early church. Why do you think it is important to know the truth? How do you know the truth?

CREEDS, COUNCILS AND CHRIST (A.D. 100-500)

After the death of the apostles, the Church Fathers (early notable church theologians) took up the mantle of leading the growing, but persecuted church. Many of these early leaders died a very painful martyr's death: being burned alive, beheaded, and eaten by lions, among other means. Because of the persecution, most Christian communities continued to worship secretly in house churches (they wouldn't begin worshiping in their own buildings until the late third century).

How does it make you feel when you are misunderstood? I know it makes me feel hurt and unappreciated. During the first several centuries of the church, many outsiders misunderstood Christian practice and worship. For example, Christians were often charged with cannibalism because they spoke of "eating the body" and "drinking the blood" of Christ (i.e. the Lord's Supper). They were charged with incest because a Christian man, for example, would marry his "sister" in

Christ. It is interesting to point out, too, that the early Christians became well-known for loving and serving one another. These were the marks of a Christian and the world was watching, which is one reason the church continued to grow!

Throughout Christian history we often find that when trouble arises through false teaching or heresy in the church, Christians have found the need to *define* themselves against the heresy. In doing this, they answer the question, "What do we believe?" The result has been a flurry of creeds, confessions, and catechisms down through the ages that testify to Christians trying to define and articulate what they believe and why they believe it. In the first several centuries of the church, *the* central issue of debate was over the person and nature of Jesus Christ, the Son of God.

Emperor Constantine

The emperor Diocletian (244-311)—who had begun an all-out persecution against Christians—divided the Roman Empire into two halves in 286: *Rome* remained the capital of the West while *Byzantium* (later renamed "Constantinople" and then renamed again to what is now Istanbul, Turkey) became the capital of the East. This division would create unforeseen consequences with a growing divide between the Western and Eastern churches, which would eventually lead to a formal split in 1054. This division is still seen today between the Roman Catholics in the West and Greek Orthodox in the East.

But something significant happened after Diocletian died. In 312, two co-emperors engaged in a battle to control the Roman Empire, Constantine and Maxentius. At one point in their conflict, Constantine (who was against Christianity) saw a vision of a sign of the Christian cross. Legend says that he also saw the words, "By this sign, you will win." That night, he had a dream of Jesus commanding him to place a Christian symbol (presumably *XP* in Greek)[1] on all his shields. Providentially, Constantine defeated Maxentius at the Battle of Milvian Bridge on October 28, 312 and credited his victory to the Christian God. That next year, in 313, Constantine issued the Edict of Milan allowing Christians to worship as they desire. Official persecution against Christians ended!

Early Ecumenical Councils

In response to various heresies and false teaching within the church, theologians and leaders have often gathered together to formulate creeds or statements of faith. One of the most prominent and notorious

---

[1] X (*chi*) and P (*rho*) are the first two letters in the word, "Christ," in Greek.

early-church heresies was *Gnosticism* [nah-sti-sizm]. Gnosticism taught that everything physical was corrupt and that only spiritual things were holy and pure. Gnostics also believed that they had received a secret knowledge[2] of God, a knowledge that translated them beyond the limitations of their corrupt physical bodies.

Because the physical world was evil, the Gnostics taught that Jesus only *appeared* to be physically human, but wasn't truly human. Thus, they were forced to reinterpret verses like John 1:14, "And the word became flesh and dwelt among us" or Colossians 2:9, "For in him the whole fullness of deity dwells bodily." Some early church leaders, like Origen (c.185-c.254), preached against Gnosticism, but ironically seemed to also incorporate various portions of its belief into their teaching. Origen even taught that God would restore all of creation—even Satan—to a sinless, spiritual state. Eventually, most Gnostics separated themselves from Christian communities.

Another notorious early-church heresy was *Arianism*. Arius (250-336), an elder from Alexandria, Egypt taught that Jesus was not fully God. Rather, God the Son was created by and subordinate to God the Father. Thus, Jesus was not eternal and a lesser being than

---

[2] The Greek word for knowledge is *gnosis*, which is the root of Gnosticism.

God the Father. This teaching is in modern-day cults like Mormonism and Jehovah's Witnesses. Arianism became so popular—spreading throughout much of Europe—that emperor Constantine convened the First Council of Nicaea in 325 to address it.

First Council of Nicaea (325)
The First Council of Nicaea proved to be a defining event in the history of the Christian church. Not only was it the first ecumenical council of the church to attain consensus through representation (outside of the council meeting in Acts 15!), it also resulted in an early form of the Nicene Creed, which is still used in many Christian worship services around the world today. Your church might even use it from time to time!

At the heart of the First Council of Nicaea was the issue of the deity of Christ. Was Jesus fully God? The result of the council—led by Athanasius (c.296-373) of Alexandria—was a clear affirmation that Jesus was both fully God and fully man; that Christ was the eternal Creator and of one substance (or essence) with the Father. Tucked away in the Nicene Creed, we find the statement, "begotten, not made," used to combat the Arian heresy. Arius himself, along with the only two representatives who didn't sign the Nicene Creed (out of about 300 in attendance), were banished to Illyria.

First Council of Constantinople (381)
While the Council of Nicaea dealt firmly with Arius and his teaching, Arianism nevertheless remained popular throughout various portions of the Roman Empire. In 380, the Roman Emperor Theodosius I (together with Emperor Gratian) made Christianity the official religion of the Roman Empire. The next year, Theodosius called a second ecumenical council in Constantinople to affirm Nicaea and to expand the affirmations to include more language about the Trinity: God the Father, God the Son, and God the Holy Spirit. Thus, a section was added to the Nicene Creed of 325 to include a portion on the Holy Spirit. This amended Nicene Creed stands as one of the greatest expressions of the Christian faith ever produced:

> *We believe in one God, the Father, the Almighty*
>
> *Maker of heaven and earth, of all that is, seen and unseen*
>
> *We believe in one Lord, Jesus Christ*
>
> *The only Son of God, eternally begotten of the Father*
>
> *God from God, Light from Light, true God from true God*
>
> *Begotten, not made, of one Being with the Father*

Through him all things were made

For us and for our salvation, he came down from heaven

By the power of the Holy Spirit

He became incarnate from the Virgin Mary, and was made man

For our sake, he was crucified under Pontius Pilate

He suffered death and was buried

On the third day he rose again, in accordance with the Scriptures

He ascended into heaven and is seated at the right hand of the Father

He will come again in glory to judge the living and the dead

And his kingdom will have no end

We believe in the Holy Spirit, the Lord, the giver of life

Who proceeds from the Father and the Son[3]

With the Father and the Son, he is worshiped and glorified

He has spoken through the prophets

We believe in one holy and apostolic Church

We acknowledge one baptism for the forgiveness of sins

We look for the resurrection of the dead and the life of the world to come

Amen

---

[3] This last phrase was added later.

The Cappadocian Fathers—Basil of Caesarea, Gregory Nazianzus, and Gregory Nyssa—became the chief defenders of Nicene orthodoxy at Constantinople and helped formulate the language on the Holy Spirit that you see toward the end of the Creed.

Council of Chalcedon (451)
Twenty years after yet another ecumenical council—the First Council of Ephesus in 431 where Nestorius (386-450) was pronounced a heretic—the Council of Chalcedon in 451 took up the issue of the natures of Christ. Chalcedon affirmed that Christ had two natures—divine and human—in one person. This union of Christ's two natures is called the "hypostatic union." Famously, they formulated the Chalcedonian Creed, which spoke of Christ's two natures being "without confusion, without change, without division, and without separation." Today, we take much of this for granted. But we should be grateful for the hard work of so many that have gone before us to hammer out what the Bible teaches about who Jesus was.

Augustine and Jerome

Among the myriads of people who had a profound influence not only during their lifetimes, but also for the centuries to follow (too many to survey in this short book!), two stand out above others: Augustine of Hippo and Jerome.

St. Augustine of Hippo (354-430)
Even though Augustine rejected Christianity early on as too simplistic and unsatisfying, his mother, Monica, began to pray for his conversion. Over time, after dabbling in Manichaeism (a form of Gnosticism), he travelled to Italy where he heard the great preacher, Ambrose of Milan. God worked through Ambrose's preaching and oriented Augustine toward the Christian faith. Ambrose would also later baptize Augustine in 387. His mother's prayers came to fruition!

Augustine wrote many well-known and influential books, including *Confessions* (the first autobiography of its kind), *The City of God* (the first philosophy of history), *On the Trinity* (a classic text on the doctrine of the Trinity), and *On Christian Doctrine* (a guide to biblical interpretation).

He also engaged in a number of highly publicized debates, most notably against Pelagius. Pelagius (c.390-418) taught that original sin did not affect human nature and, therefore, the human will can choose good or evil apart from God's grace or assistance. In response, Augustine rebuked Pelagianism—showing from Scripture that humans are dead in sin and carry the curse of the Fall of Adam (cf. Eph. 2; Gen. 3; Rom. 5). God has decreed the end from the beginning (Isa. 46), chosen a people as his own (Eph. 1), and preserves them to the end (Phil. 1). It is only by grace that anybody is saved (Eph. 2). A thousand years after Augustine breathed his last, his teachings would have a profound impact on the Protestant Reformation.

Jerome (c.345-420)

A biblical scholar, monk, historian, and theologian, Jerome became proficient in the original languages of the Bible, Hebrew and Greek. His most important achievement was the *Vulgate*, a translation from the original languages of the Bible into Latin. The *Vulgate* became the standard Bible of the Roman Catholic Church for the next 1,000 years! Latin had already taken the mantle as the "official" language of the church, in part, because it was the only language "unstained" by the injustice and treatment of Jesus (sealed on the sign above his head). The Jews (who spoke Hebrew) put him up for crucifixion and the Romans (who spoke Greek) did the deed. Latin, then, was the pure tongue of the church. Jerome also wrote many other works, making him the *second*-most voluminous writer of the period, the first being Augustine!

The history of the church between A.D. 100-500 centers on the official state sanctioning of Christianity in the fourth century and the development of the theology of the person and natures of Jesus, the Son of God. This latter point can be seen through a variety of ecumenical councils, all of which affirmed the full deity and humanity of Christ. We, today, often take for granted the doctrine of the Trinity as it is so nicely defined and articulated (e.g. Nicene Creed). But this came at a price—the defense of biblical doctrine against a raging set of heretical views. We stand on the shoulders of these men who have given the church a rich heritage of theology, faith, and passion for truth.

DISCUSSION QUESTIONS

- Why do people write creeds or confessions of faith?
- What modern-day cults downgrade Jesus to a lower being than God the Father?
- In line with St. Augustine, if a person is born "dead in sin," how can he or she be saved? Can we, of our own accord, choose salvation apart from God's gracious initiative? Why or why not?

THE CHURCH IN THE DARK AGES (A.D. 500-1000)

On a chilly October morning in 2003, I went caving in a large cave in eastern Tennessee with several friends. So we wouldn't get lost, we carved arrows into the sticky mud that blanketed the floor of the cave and set out candles along the way. After about an hour of squeezing through small cracks and crawling through small underground streams, we looked back through the stalactites and realized that we were completely lost. "Don't panic," I thought to myself.

One reality of caving is that, if you turn off your flashlight, it is pitch black. You can't even see your hand in front of your face! In that cold, dark, and damp hole beneath seventy feet of solid rock, I suddenly wanted to get out; the darkness was too much. And so, after several wrong turns, we eventually made it out. The church, too, once entered a period of darkness; what we refer to as the "Dark Ages."

In 330, Emperor Constantine moved the capital of the Roman Empire from the western city of Rome to the eastern city of Byzantium, which he then renamed "Constantinople." With this move, the city of Rome began to lose political influence to the new capital. Constantinople would remain the bastion of Christianity until 1453 when the Muslims conquered it and (later) renamed it "Istanbul." But other factors would also weaken and destroy the power and influence of the Roman Empire.

While the Middle Ages span from roughly 500 to 1500, the period between 500-1000 is often referred to as the Dark Ages because of the economic, intellectual, and spiritual deterioration across Europe and around the Mediterranean Sea. It would also witness the rise of a militaristic religion, Islam.

In addition to the destruction of Rome in the 5th century and its "light" eclipsed by war, disease, and a lack of intellectual pursuit, the church began to steer away from the Bible in its worship, ministry, and theology. Church hierarchy (from pope down to priest), an overemphasis on the sacraments to exclusion of the Bible, and internal conflicts rendered the institutional church "dark." However, the church *invisible*— the true body and bride of Christ—would continue on as the elect and remnant of God as he had planned from the beginning. Years later, during the Protestant Reformation in the 1500s, a Latin phrase would capture the essence of the Reformation spirit: *Post Tenebras Lux*, "After darkness, light!"

The Sack of Rome

Various Germanic tribes throughout Europe —collectively known as the "Goths"—began to rise in political and military power during the 4th and early 5th centuries. One of these tribes, called the *Visigoths*, attacked and sacked Rome in 410 and then headed to Spain, where they ruled until the Muslims conquered them in the early 8th century. In 455, another tribe, the *Vandals*, leveraged a devastating attack on Rome. Each of these attacks on Rome weakened it until finally, on the 4th of September 476, the Roman Empire fell to Odoacer, a Germanic chieftain.

Most of these various Germanic tribes subscribed to the Christian heretical sect of Arianism (see discussion in the last chapter), which taught that Jesus Christ was not fully God, but was God's first created being. While the Roman Empire and these Germanic tribes thought of themselves as "Christian," such a designation caused serious problems in identifying who the *true* Christians were.

Unfortunately, as is often the case, conforming to a Christian *culture* is often confused with becoming a Christian. How do you tell the difference between someone who simply conforms externally to a Christian "culture"—doing all the right things—and someone who truly believes?

The Pope and the Papacy

Today, the pope (derived from the Greek word for *father*) is the "Bishop of Rome" and leader of the Roman Catholic Church (RCC) worldwide. But this position was not always clear and the title was added after the first centuries of the church for the purposes of control, power, and "Christian" influence. In fact, it wasn't until the 11th century, that the title "pope" came to apply solely to the Bishop of Rome! The office itself grew in particular influence after the decline of the Roman Empire, as a kind of stability for the people. Tracing its roots back to the first "pope" in Rome, who the RCC believes to be the apostle Peter, the RCC takes pride in its long, uninterrupted history. But is that the *real* story?

Peter, of course, never used or bore the title "pope." Moreover, there is no evidence that Jesus appointed Peter to be the "Bishop of Rome" nor did Jesus establish the papacy. When Jesus told Peter, "On this rock I will build my church" (Matt. 16:18), the RCC takes "rock" to mean *Peter* (the Greek word for Peter is *petra*, "rock"), though, this interpretation is probably untrue. Notwithstanding, even if the RCC argues in favor of this interpretation, the issue of *papal succession* is something entirely different and not found in the pages of Scripture.

Just because Jesus designated Peter to be an early leader of the church does not give a succession of non-apostles the same kind of apostolic authority—especially to the degree that we see it today (i.e. the doctrine of papal infallibility). Moreover, at various times throughout church history (for example, during the 14th century in Avignon, France), multiple "popes" all claimed the title, while simultaneously excommunicating the other "popes" and all their followers!

But we shouldn't get the idea that all the popes were bad or evil. One of the most famous popes of the early Middle Ages was Pope Gregory I (540-604), also known as Gregory the Great. Gregory's leadership and humility became a shining light of biblical Christianity in a sea of darkness. He introduced Christian devotion, a concern for evangelism, and affirmed the importance of moral behavior. Before he became pope, Gregory lived as a monk— dedicated to imitating the life of Jesus through contemplation, service, and a disdain for worldliness. He is well known for his written work, *Book of Pastoral Rule*, in which he outlined the characteristics and marks of a minister.

A defining moment came on Christmas Day, in the year 800, when Pope Leo III crowned the king of France, Charles the Great (or *Charlemagne*), as the first Roman Emperor in more than three centuries and ruler over what would later be called the "Holy Roman Empire." Like that of the Roman Empire in 380, the church and state became one—but with the *church* crowning the emperor this time!

Charlemagne believed that the church (especially the clergy) was necessary for a well-ordered and quality-controlled society. If he wanted functional control over Europe, he must also have direct control over the church. Charlemagne also spurred church reforms and learning, even serving as the patron for a number of scholars in a wide variety of disciplines and for a number of monasteries to preserve ancient texts. One of the great legacies of Charlemagne, though, had to do with his military campaigns against the growing militant religion, Islam.

The Rise of Islam

Muhammad (c.570-632) was born in Mecca, near the western coast of modern-day Saudi Arabia, and lived there for the first fifty-two years of his life. Growing up, he was part of a local pagan religion, but had heard bits and pieces of the Old and New Testaments and, thus, wasn't all too unfamiliar with their content. In 610, while praying in a cave outside of Mecca, Muhammad supposedly received a revelation from the angel Gabriel (the same angel who appeared to the Virgin Mary). Over a period of time, he would continue to receive these revelations, which would later be compiled into the *Qur'an*, the sacred book of Islam.

After ten years of preaching, several hundred families had become convinced that Muhammad was a prophet of the one God, Allah. Still a minority religion, he and his followers faced persecution and they eventually fled Mecca for the city of Medina in 622. Muhammad and his small (but growing) clan brutally took control of Medina through a series of bloody battles. Then, in 630—with an army of 10,000 men at his command—he returned to Mecca, conquered it, and dedicated it to Allah.

Suddenly, in 632, Muhammad died from illness in the arms of Aisha, who was one of his twelve wives. He had married Aisha when she was only six years of age and consummated the marriage when she was only nine. Apparently, the Qur'an's limit to four wives didn't apply to him (cf. Qur'an, Sura 4:3)!

As soon as Muhammad died, his followers split into two groups over who should succeed him as their leader, the Sunnis and the Shi'ites. The Sunnis believed that his successor should be elected democratically while the Shi'ites believed that his successor should be related to Muhammad. Disagreements and even warfare between these two groups continue even to this day (by the way, there are currently about 150 sects of Islam).

It is hard to underestimate the significance of the rise of Islam when we consider the history of the church. Within only the first century after Muhammad's death—by the early 700s—Muslims had conquered the holy land (modern-day Israel), North Africa, southern France and Spain, and parts of central Asia. If it were not for several crucial victories in Europe—notably, the victory by Charles Martel at the Battle of Tours in 732—all of Europe might have fallen to the Muslims as well.

The Dark Ages was a period of warfare, intellectual and spiritual decline, and power struggles within the church. By the year 1000, two major issues came to a head. First, the threat of Islam continued to put pressure on maintaining a Christian Europe. Second, the Eastern and Western parts of the Church were drifting further and further apart. Both of these, as we shall see, would have lasting implications.

DISCUSSION QUESTIONS

- What is meant by the phrase "the Dark Ages"?
- How do you tell if a professing Christian is merely conforming to a Christian "culture" or if he or she truly believes?
- Where did the idea of the Catholic "Pope" come from? Do you see any solid basis for this position from the Bible?
- At what point in Muhammad's life did he really become violent? Why do you think so many today do *not* consider Islam a religion of peace?

DIVIDE AND CONQUER
(A.D. 1000-1300)

If you've talked with many atheists, agnostics, or maybe even friends who oppose the Christian faith, you've probably heard them refer to the "Crusades" as an example of how Christianity can be violent at times. It's a valid point. You've maybe heard, too, how divisive churches can be, which is why we see so many denominations and a splintering of "Christian" groups around the world. Again, another valid point. How would you answer these criticisms? Let's take a look at what happened.

As mentioned in the last chapter, two major issues came to a head by the year 1000: (1) the church was growing further and further apart between the East and West (and not by distance!) and (2) the militant spread of Islam was continuing to conquer peoples and lands. Both of these would have deep and lasting consequences. Additionally, the church's theology and worship continued to develop along with its method of learning new things. Whether we realize it or not, we see traces of what happened between A.D. 1000 and 1300 all around us today.

The Split Between East and West

If you recall (from Chapter 3), part of the Nicene Creed states, "We believe in the Holy Spirit, the Lord, the giver of life, who proceeds from the Father *and the Son.*" This last phrase, "and the Son," sparked considerable controversy between the Bishop of Rome and the Bishop of Constantinople (the Western and Eastern capitals, respectively). Why?

Some say that a single word doesn't mean too much, but during the 8th century, a church in Spain added one little Latin word to the Nicene Creed, *Filioque* ("and the Son"). That one little word sparked a huge division! *Filioque* emphasized the fact that Jesus Christ is fully God in his own right—his deity is not derived from God the Father. This view, endorsed by the Western theologians (based in Rome), understood the divine being to dwell *equally* in the Father, Son, and Holy Spirit. The Eastern theologians (based in Constantinople), on the other hand, believed that the Father shares his divine being with the Son and Spirit. Thus, the Eastern Church would not confess that the Spirit proceeds from the Father *and the Son.* It seems like a small issue, but it characterized how the two sides viewed who God is, which is not a small issue. Was God the Father more "God" than God the Son or God the Spirit?

In 872, the pope (Bishop of Rome) agreed to drop the phrase "and the Son" only if the Eastern churches acknowledged the pope's absolute supremacy over all Christendom. The Bishop of Constantinople, Photius, was offended at his "offer" and the gap between the East and West grew wider.

Then, in the summer of 1054, Pope Leo IX issued a papal bull (a formal declaration and notice) of various "unacceptable" practices of the Eastern Church, such as allowing priests to marry and not recognizing baptisms performed in the Western Church. This led to both sides issuing letters of excommunications against the other.[1] Thus, 1054 is considered the year of the official break between what would be called the Roman Catholic Church and the Eastern Orthodox Church, a break that has continued to the present day.

Monks and Monasteries

In a rather unfazed manner, clusters of Christians throughout Europe gathered together with differing agendas and vows. Many of these houses or "monasteries"

---

[1] "Excommunication" is a formal declaration of church discipline by the church stating that the offending person is no longer in communion with the church and, therefore, with Christ.

became centers of education and service. Monks became a standard addition to the Christian church in the early 4th century. Famous monks down through history— Anthony of Egypt (251-356), Augustine of Hippo (354-430), Anthony the Hermit (c.468-c.520), Benedict (c.480-543), Bernard of Clairvaux (1090-1153), Bruno of Cologne (c.1030-1101), Francis of Assisi (1181/1182-1226), and Dominic de Guzmán (1170-1221)—have each made a lasting impression on both ancient and modern-day religious orders and monastic communities. Today, there are hundreds of monasteries and religious orders all around the world. Many of them intentionally separate themselves from the world to be devoted to study, prayer, contemplation, and service. Can you think of any benefits of this way of living?

The Crusades (1095-1291)

Since the rise of Islam in the 7th century, the Muslims had militarily conquered the historic Christian cities and lands, significantly Jerusalem. Pope Urban II (1042-1099) called a special council together in 1095—the Council of Clermont—to address the possibility of re-taking those lands back from the Muslims. The people approved with *Deus vult* ("God will it!") and for the next four months, emissaries travelled all over Europe for the purpose of recruiting soldiers.

The response was tremendous! Kings and nobles, peasants and foot soldiers all joined the mission. Many of these recruits were previous enemies and had even been at war with each other! But none of that mattered anymore; they were intent on re-taking the land for Christ and (for some) getting a free pass to heaven from the pope.

When Urban II launched the First Crusade in 1095, little did he know that it would end in a 200-year failure. From 1095 to 1291, Christians throughout Europe engaged in a total of *seven* major crusades and numerous smaller battles. While the intentions of some might have been grand—many believing they were setting out on a holy pilgrimage—their actions throughout the conflict were less so. It was a dark period in the history of the church and unlike the Muslims—who acted according to teachings of the Qur'an—many of the Crusaders did *not* act according to the teachings of the Bible.

The Crusaders took back Jerusalem, but the Muslims again recaptured it, and so it went. But the Muslims weren't the only ones who received the brutal treatment at the hands of the Crusaders. Jews and other non-Christians were also slaughtered, burned, and pillaged. After the Crusaders were defeated during the Third Crusade (1189-1192), Pope Innocent III rallied for a fourth try. Interestingly, merchants in Venice agreed to supply the next army with ships at the cost of 84,000 silver coins. However, only one-third of the expected number of Crusaders showed up and they were 34,000 coins short! How would they pay for the ships?

A wealthy Eastern prince offered to supply the remaining amount under one condition: the Crusaders had to travel to Constantinople and dethrone the emperor (who he obviously didn't like). After arriving in Constantinople, and several minor skirmishes with the people of the city, the "Christian" Crusaders sacked the "Christian" Constantinople on Good Friday, 1204. They raped and killed innocent civilians, tore down Christian statues, and took over the city. All dreams of having the Western and Eastern Churches reunited were dashed to pieces, along with the rest of the city. Another reason that the Crusades have left a dark legacy on Christian history.

Transubstantiation

While Innocent III's rally for the Fourth Crusade fell on rocky ground, he would make a much more lasting contribution to the development of Roman Catholic worship. In 1215, Innocent called together the Fourth Lateran Council, which turned out to be the culminating event of his reign. Out of the many laws passed, three in particular were of great significance: (1) a lengthy explanation of the sacrament of Communion, (2) an affirmation of the primacy of the pope, and (3) the foundation of what would be called the "Inquisition," a church-ordered tribunal concerned with detection and prosecution of theological heresy.

While the second and third laws are self-explanatory, the first one became the standard expression of how the Roman Catholic Church understood the sacrament of Holy Communion. They said: "[Christ's] body and blood are contained in the sacraments under the outward forms of bread and wine; the bread being *transubstantiated* by God's power into the body, and the wine into the blood."

In other words—according to Roman Catholic theology—when you take the bread and wine in Communion, you actually take the physical body and blood of Christ even though the elements don't *look* and *taste* like a real body and blood. This doctrine, called *transubstantiation*, has defined the central act of Roman Catholic worship ever since. In Latin, the final farewell of the Communion service is "*missa est*," which means "Go forth." Catholics then began calling their Communion service *missa* or *Mass*, which continues to this day.

Scholasticism

"Scholasticism" is a big word, but describes a very important movement beginning in the late 11th century that would last for several centuries. Scholastics (as they became known) took ancient and "authoritative" texts and found what seemed like contradictory statements. They then tried to prove—by the rules of simple logic—that these ancient texts were in fact *not* contradictory. Thus, they advanced the idea of an underlying agreement of the religious texts of the church. Scholasticism became the primary method of learning in schools and universities and lasted until the 16th century!

A number of influential theologians and philosophers developed aspects of the scholastic method. Anselm (1033-1109)—who became well-known for his argument for the existence of God—and Peter Abelard (1079-1142) both continued to develop various aspects of learning with the rules of logic.

Scholastics believed that asking questions was the primary means of arriving at the truth. During the 13th century, various schools across Europe began developing their own "brand" of Scholasticism. Peter Lombard's (1100-1160) *Sentences* became a primary textbook for many of the schools across Europe and it was Lombard who gave to the Roman Catholic Church (RCC) the official list of seven sacraments that are still held by the RCC today (baptism, Eucharist, penance, confirmation, marriage, ordination, and last rights).

While all of these men made significant contributions to the development of theology and thought, the most important theologian and philosopher of the scholastic period— and of the Middle Ages—was Thomas Aquinas (1225-1274). Aquinas' watershed book on theology and philosophy, *Summa Theologiae*, is without question one of the most influential works of Western literature and served as a primary source for all of the main teachings of the RCC.

Aquinas not only laid much of the groundwork for later Roman Catholic theology, he also prioritized those parts of its theology within Roman Catholic theology. For example, he argued that Holy Communion was the highest of the sacraments and articulated a detailed and highly philosophical explanation of the doctrine of transubstantiation. He also recovered the perceived importance of Aristotelian natural philosophy; namely, that there was no fundamental contra- diction between the works of God and the natural world. Aquinas' teaching of theology, doctrine, the sacraments, and philosophy—as summarized in his *Summa*—shaped Catholic thought thereafter.

Scholasticism came to a halt when people like Duns Scotus (c.1265-1308) and William of Ockham (c.1285-1347) started to decry the "supremacy" of logic used in the scholastic method. They argued that the structure of the world (i.e., its "logic") was only one of many possible manifestations of God's power and, ultimately, logic should be confined to the area of *words* only, not to the realities those words represent. The Humanists, too, began attacking the scholastic method for their perceived pragmatism. They believed, rather, that people should study the *humanities*: poetry, grammar, rhetoric, history, and philosophy. These combined criticisms crippled the scholastic movement, which eventually lost its central method in universities by the 16th century.

The turbulent years between 1000 and 1300 shaped both the secular and religious world thereafter. By the end of 1300, the Roman Catholic and Greek Orthodox Churches stood opposed to each other and many had died at the hands of both Muslims and Christians. When the dust settled, an organized Catholic theology brought some sense of unity out of the chaos but, as we shall see in the next chapter, that unity was on the brink of shattering once again.

DISCUSSION QUESTIONS

- How would you respond to an atheist who says, "Well, your religion isn't a religion of peace, just look at what you Christians did during the Crusades!"?
- Why did the Eastern and Western Churches split? Was that a good decision or not?
- Can you imagine what the life of a monk might look like? What's the first thing that comes to your head when you hear the word, "monk"?
- If you had to describe the Roman Catholic view of Communion, what would you say? How is that different from what you might believe about it?

THE ROAD TO THE REFORMATION (A.D. 1300-1500)

A plethora of streams, creeks, and rivers riddle the Easter United States. As a kid, I grew up rafting and (later in life) kayaking down many of these. The chilly water and raging rapids seemed to quench my quest for adventure! Like most places around the world, these creeks and rivers converge into bigger creeks and rivers. Sometimes they pool into lakes and other times they empty into the oceans.

By 1500, a number of streams and creeks had converged into a raging torrent that would spark the Protestant Reformation. These include: social anxieties across Europe, issues related to church authority, the moral failures and abuses of priests, a growing desire for spiritual devotion, and a call to go back to the authentic biblical documents. All of these would have a role to play in one of the most significant events of church history, the Protestant Reformation.

Social Anxieties

Several social anxieties elicited a greater awareness of spiritual matters and the afterlife. You could say (as some have argued) that there was a preoccupation with fate and death. In 1319, a severe famine hit. Many starved to death and even criminals were taken from the gallows and fed to the poor in Poland and other parts of Europe. One of the most devastating events of the 14th century was the Bubonic Plague or "Black Death." Between 1348 and 1352, it is estimated that anywhere from one-third to one-half of the entire European population died as a direct result of the plague.

The Black Death produced a shortage of workers, and with a shortage of workers, potential employers had to increase wages to attract them. The effect was that this gave the workers an added sense of expectations and "rights." Even the peasant-worker suddenly felt a sense of "worth"—that he deserved higher wages and better working conditions. Over time, this led to a general questioning of authority, especially *church* authority (as we will later see, this is one of the reasons why many of Luther's followers were peasants).

There was also a close connection between this anxiety and fear of death and the sense of guilt. Death implied God's judgment and judgment brought a sinner face to face with God's holiness and wrath. Some travelled from town to town whipping themselves with leather scourges in hopes of atoning for their sins and for the sins of others. The Roman Catholic Church fueled the fear of hell through pamphlets and drawings and the priests exploited these fears by speaking of what hell was like so as to raise funds for their immoral escapades and lavish living.

Out of fear, many turned to visions and superstitious stories for comfort. During this time, a significant population turned to witchcraft! In fact, by 1484, there were so many witches that Pope Innocent VIII began an Inquisition to stamp out any witchcraft in Europe. This started a scary "witch hunt," which subjected countless women (especially single women) to unspeakable torture and execution. By the early 1600s, some 30,000 women were executed for witchcraft!

Spiritual Devotion

Relatively few, of course, turned their quest for spiritual things toward witchcraft and false spirituality. Most sought an intimate fellowship with the triune God and *mysticism* became a popular form of individual spirituality. One type of mysticism emphasized the human will's conformity to the will of God through successive stages of purgation of sin, illumination by the Spirit, and contemplation on holy texts. Thomas à Kempis' (1380-1471) *The Imitation of Christ* is a popular example of this strand of mysticism.

Another type of mysticism believed each individual shared a spark of the divine and had the possibility of full union with God himself. This mystical union with God was achieved by letting go of one's self, a detachment from the worldly desires. Both of these types of mysticism tended to discredit the hierarchy of the church. Moreover, church leaders seemed too worldly, too man-centered.

Church Authority

One of the major issues leading to the Protestant Reformation had to do with the extent of the church's authority. The pope's laws often interfered with the local kings and lords of various lands across Europe. The problem that many of these local rulers had was that, while they wanted to limit Pope's authority, they also wanted the pope to *manage* the churches within their lands.

Moreover, the question arose: who should judge certain "sins" if those sins infringed on *both* church *and* state? Over time, the pope's actual power began to wane before the power of local kings. As more and more local kings appointed their own bishops and priests, those bishops and priests would be loyal—not to the pope—but to the king who appointed them and provided their income!

At one point, the pope became ruler of the Italian army, which defeated other local rulers in northern Italy and Europe—the people of which were members of the Roman Catholic Church and who were paying their tithe money to the Roman Catholic Church. Oftentimes, the pope was more Italian than church! Most popes and cardinals were Italian, which began to seem suspicious in an age of increasing sovereign states. In fact, from 1400-1978 only two popes were *not* Italian and one of those only ruled for two years! The question arose: what was the value of a pope's excommunication against a king resisting aggression by the pope's army? It became a lose-lose situation.

Another issue related to church authority had to do with how people became priests or bishops. The Church accepted payment for offices or positions (called simony). Some church officials were showing favoritism toward relatives in procuring positions rather than objective evaluation and qualification (called nepotism). All of these factors together weakened the foundation of the

Roman Catholic Church's authority. But these certainly weren't the only ones.

Moral Corruption and Indulgences

At the time, the Church expected regular contributions from all their subjects from across Europe, but those subjects didn't see how their money was being used for good purposes. All they saw was abuse: simony, nepotism, scandal, murder, drunkards, theft, lavish living, clergy concubines, etc. and no accountability or discipline!

This last point is key. The church didn't discipline its own ministers, which was scandalous in the eyes of the people. During this time, too, many lay people faced excommunication if they didn't pay their contribution to the church! Because of this, monastic communities—pledged to poverty— became very popular. Clergy abuse by 1500 wasn't really any worse than in 1300, but more people became *aware* of it. By 1500, the church began to outspend itself and desperately needed money for the building of St. Peter's in Rome. How did the church raise money? Indulgences.

An indulgence—a remission of sin granted when the sinner pays a certain amount of money to the church—was one of a number of non-biblical duties pushed on the people; others being pilgrimages, superstitious relics, prayers to the Virgin Mary, and Masses.

To generate money, the church needed to increase awareness of the peoples' guilt before a God of wrath so that they would do *anything*—preferably pay a sum of money!— to "pay" for their sins. This led to a ceaseless effort to earn merit before God! Once a sinner confessed his sin, he still needed to pay for an indulgence or do works of penance to earn merit as a way of paying for that sin.

Morning Stars

Another stream leading into the Reformation River were the voices of several pre-Reformers or "morning stars" of the Reformation, particularly, John Wycliffe (1320-1384) and John Huss (c.1372-1415). An English theologian and lay preacher, Wycliffe took the lead in translating the Scriptures from the Latin Vulgate into English, now known as the *Wycliffe Bible*. Though brought up on charges several times, he always seemed to escape the penalties of the state (including execution). He suffered a stroke and died in 1384.

John Huss, inspired by Wycliffe's teachings, became a Bohemian Reformer and preacher in Prague. Both Wycliffe and Huss opposed the church hierarchy of their day, pointing out its many abuses and scandals.

Huss believed there to be many people—even the pope himself—who were simply part of the visible, external church while not being a part of the true ("invisible") church, which is God's elect. Wycliffe and Huss both emphasized preaching, studying the Scriptures, and eliminating clerical abuses.

The Roman Catholic Church condemned both men. In 1415 Huss was burned at the stake and, in 1428, Wycliffe's bones were exhumed and burned as well.

Back to the Sources!

Like a faster-moving current of water, several other pre-reformation streams started to gain momentum. One of these was the use of the printing press, invented by Johann Gutenberg in the 1450s. Francis Bacon (1561-1626) would later say that the three greatest inventions of "recent history" were gunpowder, the mariner's compass, and printing.

It must be remembered that, at the time, books were extremely expensive because they had to be written by hand. The printing press changed that forever. Gutenberg printed the Bible in 1454 and by 1500 there were some 250 print shops across Europe. Over 100 editions of the Bible were released between 1457 and 1500. Later, at the spark of the Reformation—during the three-year span from 1517 to 1520—Martin Luther's writings sold more than 300,000 copies, attesting to the ground swell of popularity. By the time of Luther's death in 1546, there was an estimated half a million copies of the Bible in circulation! As a result of the printing press, more and more people became literate and many began reading and writing.

In 1453, Constantinople fell to the Muslims and the Greek-speaking theologians were forced to leave the East, many being dispersed throughout Europe. Significantly, they brought with them vast amounts of ancient Greek literature, including Greek manuscripts and texts of the New Testament.

In Europe, the humanist movement was taking off, especially among intellectuals. Humanism (not the secular humanism of today!) was a way of learning based upon the recovery of classical sources of Roman, Greek, and Christian literature. Their motto: *Ad fonts*, which meant "back to the sources." Rather than taking the church's word for it, more and more people wanted to see the ancient and biblical texts for themselves, as many could now read thanks to the printing press.

As a result, they affirmed that Scripture, not the pope, was the final authority. The famous example of this came when a man named Lorenzo Valla (1407-1457) came upon the word *metanoia* in Matthew 4:17 from the Greek New Testament. He compared it to Jerome's Latin Vulgate translation— the standard version of the Roman Catholic Church at the time—which rendered the word, "do penance." As noted earlier, the practice of penance was a system of meriting righteousness before God by doing good works. Valla challenged this translation, insisting that the word should be translated *repentance*, not "do penance." Repentance, Valla argued, referred to a genuine change of heart and mind rather than the ritual performance required by the sacrament of penance.

When Erasmus (1466-1536), the most well known humanist, issued his 1516 edition of the Greek New Testament, he incorporated Valla's translation of *metanoia* over Jerome's. Martin Luther, in turn, used Erasmus' translation of "repentance" in his Ninety-five Theses, which sparked the Protestant Reformation in 1517. It was said, as early as 1520, "Erasmus laid the egg that Luther hatched." Erasmus later replied that Luther's chicks were a different kind of bird!

Erasmus was the *New York Times* bestseller of his day. Everybody was reading Erasmus. His witty, humorous, scholarly, and piercing critiques of the church and its abuses hit home with the masses across Europe. Erasmus articulated in print what everyone was thinking, but had a hard time verbalizing—his words resonated with public opinion. He not only lowered the reputation of popes, cardinals, and bishops, but also of the Roman Catholic theologians, weakening the foundations of their theology and authority.

Greek, Hebrew, and Latin became popular and were incorporated into the universities and seminaries across Europe. It became so popular that, in 1478, the Spanish Inquisition condemned the study of these ancient texts because it was bringing more and more suspicion upon the theological foundation of the Roman Catholic Church!

With the newly-invented printing press, the humanists could now publish their works inexpensively and distribute them on a large scale. They even went back to the early Church Fathers—St. Augustine of Hippo in particular—and re-discovered their wisdom and insight. You could say that the 15th to 17th centuries were kind of an "Augustinian Renaissance." In fact, Martin Luther became an Augustinian monk and John Calvin quotes him more than any other author in his famous *Institutes of the Christian Religion*!

All told, the humanists revived learning. The new learning revived suspicions of church order and tradition. These suspicions led to opposition. The only thing needed was for someone to come along—from the inside—who would lead reform. From local pubs across Europe to the universities, the call to reform the church seeped into popular songs, poetry, pubs, drinking ditties, and even university lectures. On the eve of the Reformation, by 1500, there was certainly not unity within the Church; it was, what one historian has called, a "pregnant plurality."

DISCUSSION QUESTIONS

- Can you imagine living through the horrifying events surrounding the Bubonic Plague? Would the threat of catching disease encourage you or discourage you in caring for the sick?

- What are three or four of the "streams" mentioned in this chapter that converged into the Reformation River? Do any stand out as especially significant?

- What do you think the impact of the printing press was on changing a whole population's perception on an issue? Would the Internet and social media have some of the same effects today?

THE CONTINENTAL REFORMATION (A.D. 1500-1600)

The Protestant Reformation was a series of theological, political, and church-related movements during the 16th century that eventually formed a split from the Roman Catholic Church. While there are a number of differences between Roman Catholic and Protestant Churches, by and large Protestant churches are those committed (1) to the authority of Scripture over tradition and the teaching of the church, (2) to justification by faith alone rather than works, and (3) the two sacraments of baptism and the Lord's Supper.

From a bird's-eye view, historians typically differentiate between the "Continental Reformation"—meaning the collective reformations that took place on the European Continent proper—and the English and Scottish Reformations. While Martin Luther is considered to be the one who actually started the Reformation in 1517, he was simply the right person at the right time, the missing component in the engine.

Luther and Calvin

Thus, it should be emphasized that many reformers took up the mantle of preaching, writing, and calling for reform of the Roman Catholic Church. Even still, a survey of church history would be incomplete without some attention to two champions of the Christian faith: Martin Luther and John Calvin.

Martin Luther (1483-1546)

Luther was born on 10 November 1483 in Eisleben, Germany. After attending various Latin schools, he enrolled at the University of Erfurt in 1501 at the age of 19. He received his master's degree four years later and entered law school. However, in 1505 as he was travelling to university, a thunderstorm stopped him in his tracks. Fearing for his life, he vowed that if he were spared, he would commit himself to the service of God. He immediately became an Augustinian monk.

As a monk, Luther sought to break free from a sense of inner despair and the fear of God's wrath. He confessed his sin—down to the nitty, gritty details—to his overseer, Johann Von Staupitz. Still nothing seemed to work. In 1508, Staupitz sent him to teach moral philosophy at the newly-founded University of Wittenberg. Three years later, in 1511, he became a professor of biblical theology, a position he held until his death.

One day, while studying the book of Romans, he came to see that his righteous standing and justification before God didn't come through performing good works, but as a gift received by *faith alone*. In other words, our righteousness has been earned by Another, Jesus Christ! On October 13, 1517, Luther nailed his Ninety-five Theses (statements of faith) to the church door in Wittenberg, which was a customary practice at that time.

Luther taught that justification came by faith *alone*, apart from works. He also decried the sale of indulgences by the Roman Catholic Church to raise money for St. Peter's, even debating the popular Catholic theologian Johann Eck in 1519 over this very issue! Moreover, Luther affirmed the authority of Scripture over the pope, over the teaching of the church, and over church tradition—what we call, the doctrine of *Sola Scriptura*.

Within the next few days after Luther posted his Ninety-five Theses, his supporters removed them, translated them from Latin into German, and then copied, printed, and distributed them all over Germany! Before long, Luther emerged as a leader of the Reformation movement that was spreading across Europe.

In 1521, the Church asked him to appear at the Diet (which means "assembly") of

Worms—in Worms, Germany—so that he would recant his writings. Refusing to do so, they declared Luther an outlaw. On his departure from Worms, he was captured by friendlies for protection at the command of the Prince of Saxony and taken to Wartburg Castle. There, he translated the Bible into his native language, German.

Luther married a former nun, Catherine von Bora, and established a model for the Christian family. He wrote many books, including his famous *The Bondage of the Will* (1525), which attacked some of Erasmus' teaching on original sin and salvation. God saved sinners, Luther argued, by grace alone, through the work of Christ alone, received by faith alone, and all to the glory of God alone!

Even though Luther eventually parted ways with another Reformer, Ulrich Zwingli (1484-1531)—over the nature of the Lord's Supper—he continued to write and preach the gospel until his death in 1546. Today, we see his legacy in his books, sermons, confessions (like the Augsburg Confession of 1530), and in the well-known hymn, "A Mighty Fortress is Our God."

John Calvin (1509-1564)
Calvin is arguably the greatest and most significant theologian in church history. Not only did his ideas shape more people,

movements, and cultures than anybody else of his day, they *directly* shaped them more than anybody else for at least the next one hundred years.

Born in 1509 in France, Calvin was known for his efforts of reform in Geneva, Switzerland. Originally a lawyer, Calvin broke with the Roman Catholic Church around 1530 and three years later was forced to leave Paris because of his Protestant convictions. He fled to Basel, Switzerland, where he wrote the first edition of what would become his most famous and influential work, *The Institutes of the Christian Religion*, in 1536.

Passing through Geneva later that year, he was persuaded by William Farel (1489-1565) to stay to help organize and continue the Reformation there. Calvin reluctantly agreed and so began a long ministry—interspersed by a brief period of exile to Strasbourg—in Geneva. He desired to see a faithful ministry of the Bible, the sacraments of baptism and the Lord's Supper, and church discipline carried out in the city. At times, the church and state were so interrelated that it was difficult to distinguish the two, especially when it came to suppressing heresy or moral corruption.

Calvin has been criticized for his role in the death of a man named Servetus, an anti-Trinitarian campaigner who was charged for heresy and burned at the stake in 1553. However, the decision didn't rest upon Calvin, but upon a council of twenty-five people. Calvin didn't want Servetus to die, but to repent and recant! Moreover, by that point, the Roman Catholic Church had already set a price on Servetus' head. Even when Servetus was sentenced to die, Calvin tried to move that he be executed by the less-painful method of beheading.

In addition to his many books and biblical commentaries, Calvin wrote five major Latin editions of his *Institutes,* one French edition, and supervised the writing of three other French editions. His final Latin edition of 1559 is five times the length of his first edition in 1536 and has become the standard edition from which most modern translations and references are made.

The central concern of Calvin's theology is union with Christ, taken root and displayed in a life of godliness (or *pietas*, in Latin). Grace displayed in the saving work of Jesus Christ, then, is central in Calvin's theology. Calvin also argued for what has been called the "third use" of God's law. If one use is to restrain sin and another to convict the sinner of his sin, then the third use of God's law points us to that which pleases

God. According to Calvin, God's laws reflect his holiness and the more one studies and attains the knowledge of God, the more he will attain the knowledge of self.

Calvin also developed other areas of biblical theology, such as the doctrine of the person and work of the Holy Spirit, the "spiritual presence" of Christ in the Lord's Supper, the role of biblical elders, and the importance of seeing Scripture through the lens of a series of relationships between God and his people—called "covenants"—from Old to New Testament.

The Five "Solas"

Reformed Theology may be summarized by ten statements of faith, which were affirmed in response to and in opposition to Roman Catholic theology.[1] Virtually all Protestant Churches (even today) accept the first five, often referred to as the "Five Solas." These five are:

1. *Sola Scriptura* – The Bible alone is the only source of authority for faith, doctrine, and Christian living.

2. *Sola Fide* – We are justified, declared "righteous" before God by faith alone, and not by works.

---

[1] For an overview of Reformed Theology, see Brian Cosby, *Rebels Rescued: A Student's Guide to Reformed Theology* (Ross-Shire, Scotland: Christian Focus Publications, 2012).

3. *Sola Gratia* – We are saved by God's grace alone, shown in the glorious gospel of Jesus Christ and applied by the Holy Spirit.

4. *Solus Christus* – There is salvation in no one else but Jesus Christ, the only Mediator between God and man.

5. *Soli Deo Gloria* – All glory and honor is due to God alone and to no other.

What's with "Tulip"?

In addition to the *Five Solas*, Reformed theology also affirms what has been referred to as the "Five Points of Calvinism" or TULIP, which is an acronym for:

1. *Total Depravity* – Man, because of his sinful nature, is born into this world dead in sin, enslaved to its services, and inclined toward evil continually.

2. *Unconditional Election* – God's sovereign choice of his people from before the foundation of the world is not dependent upon man's decision or will, but upon God's free grace.

3. *Limited Atonement* – Christ came to purposefully and intentionally die for God's elect, his people.

4. *Irresistible Grace* – God, by his Spirit, effectually calls, regenerates, and saves sinners by grace alone.

5. *Perseverance of the Saints* – Once a person is saved, he or she will always be saved; true salvation cannot be lost.

TULIP is often mistakenly attributed to John Calvin. To be sure, they are drawn from Calvin's theology (and before him, from the Bible!), but it was the Dutch Reformed Church at the Synod of Dordt that arranged these five points in 1618-1619 in opposition to Jacobus Arminius' (1560-1609) "five points." All ten articles of faith—the Five Solas and TULIP—present an ordered expression of biblical theology. They also present a decidedly God-centered view of the world rather than a man-centered view of the world.

The Outcome?

It would be nice to say that everything was settled after the Reformers split from the Roman Catholic Church, but that is far from the truth. Years of deadly battles, wars, and reforms shaped the political and religious landscape not only in Europe, but also around the world. The Roman Catholic Church responded to the "heresies" of the Protestants in the Council of Trent (1545-1563) while the Protestant Church began to splinter into various groups, denominations, and movements.

One of these movements, called the Radical Reformation, formed a paradoxical identity of being both pacifist *and* militaristic, depending on which branch of it you came across. Its leaders, people like Menno Simons (and his followers, the Mennonites) and Thomas Müntzer seemed to capture both of these extremes. One of the better-known branches of the Radical Reformation was the Anabaptists, who (as their name suggests) required members to be baptized *again*— as they were all, at that point, baptized as infants—and became heavily persecuted for their "radical" differences from the Roman Catholic Church.

By 1600, many of the major theological and church-related shifts of the Reformation had taken place. Courses were, for the most part, set and the world would never be the same. This can be seen from the rise of Reformed churches, Lutheran churches, Anglican churches, and a variety of Anabaptist and Radical Reformation movements. All of these would, together, be categorized under the umbrella term, "Protestant." But, for our intents and purposes in this overview, we need to back up and consider the impact of the Reformation in England and Scotland.

DISCUSSION QUESTIONS

- According to the Reformers, how are we (as sinners) accepted by a holy God? Where does our righteousness come from?
- What does *sola Scriptura* mean? Why is the issue of authority so crucial when it comes to solving problems in the church today?
- Where did the "five points of Calvin" come from? What do you think most people think of Calvin today?
- All of the Protestant denominations stem, in their present form, from the Reformation. What are some commonalities between all (or most) Protestant denominations?

THE ENGLISH REFORMATION AND THE PURITANS (A.D. 1500-1700)

Many biology classes use an organic compound called formaldehyde to preserve specimens—frogs, worms, and larger animals—for dissection. The worst part about formaldehyde is its pungent odor (one that's hard to forget!). After examining the parts of a frog one day in my biology class, I carried its irritating scent with me all day! Friends avoided me, girls avoided me (which was rather typical), and I wanted to avoid me too! All I could think about that day was trying to get rid of the lingering scent.

In a similar way, reformers during the later 16th century and their supporters during the 17th century wanted to get rid of the remaining vestiges of Roman Catholicism in the church. To many, it was a putrefying odor and they wanted to *purify* the church from corruption, unbiblical theology, and idolatrous worship.

The Reformation had a profound impact in England and Scotland, which in turn had a greater impact on the establishment of the New World. Unlike the Continental

Reformation, the English Reformation began not with a grass-roots campaign and a monk, but at the top, with the king!

At risk of oversimplifying the period between 1500 and 1700, the first half can roughly be identified with the actual events of the English Reformation, while the second half is often called the *Post-Reformation*— the theological, pastoral, social, and political outworking of the Reformation.

Christianity in England

England has had a long Christian heritage, dating back to probably the early 2nd century. British bishops attended the Council of Arles in 314, which gives evidence to an organized church in England by that point.

In 597, Pope Gregory the Great sent Augustine of Canterbury (*not* St. Augustine of Hippo!) to Christianize the Kingdom of Kent and convert the people from Anglo-Saxon paganism (the Anglo-Saxons were a group of Germanic tribes who had migrated there in the 5th century). Within a few months, King Ethelbert of Kent adopted the Christian faith and many of the people followed suit, like a game of Follow-the-Leader. Later on, in 668, Theodore of Tarsus (c.602-690) set about organizing the church in England into various clusters and summoning large-scale church councils. Much of what we know about early Christian history in England comes from Venerable Bede (c.673-735) in his book, *The Ecclesiastical History of the English People*, completed in 731.

The Christian king, Alfred the Great (849-499), who ruled the area of Wessex in Southern England, famously defended the English people from Viking invasions and became the dominant ruler in England. He was regarded as a model of what a Christian king should be—promoting Christian learning and even translating popular works from Latin into English (i.e. *Pastoral Rule* by Gregory the Great). Alfred's reign increasingly solidified the identity of England as a Christian nation.

Throughout the Middle Ages, the church in England continued to be subject to the Roman Catholic Church. By the 13th century, papal power in England had become very great. However, with a strengthening national pride and a growing awareness of scandals in the church, more and more people in England began to criticise Roman Catholic control. This was during a time when the church in Rome began asking for increasing amounts of money from its constituents in England.

Until the 1500s, English translations of the Bible were forbidden; the Latin Vulgate was the "official" translation. However, the work of John Wycliffe (see last chapter) and

William Tyndale (1490-1536) began to shake this foundation with their translations of the Bible into English. Often called the "Father of the English Bible," Tyndale was the first to translate the Bible from the original Hebrew and Greek into English for the general public (Wycliffe had translated it from Latin). In 1535, Miles Coverdale (c.1488-1569) published the first *complete* English translation, much of the work being Tyndale's.

With the help of Thomas Cranmer (1489-1556)—then Archbishop of Canterbury and later author of the Book of Common Prayer—every parish church in England would soon have a copy of the English Bible!

Henry VIII and the Church of England

As mentioned earlier, the English Reformation began from the top, with the king himself, but not because he liked Luther or believed in Reformed theology! The moment came when King Henry VIII (1491-1547) wanted an annulment with his wife, Catherine of Aragon, so that he could marry Ann Boleyn (he would go on to have a total of *six wives* before his death). When the pope refused the annulment, Henry separated the church *in* England from the Roman Catholic Church in 1534 and declared himself as the "Supreme Head of the Church *of* England," even though he was theologically opposed to Protestantism.

The theological and church-related changes were introduced only after Henry died and his son, Edward VI (1537-1553), ascended the throne. Edward was only nine years old when he became King of England and, therefore, ruled under the authority of a Council, with Thomas Cranmer taking the lead for church reform. During Edward's short reign—and under Cranmer's leadership—the Church of England changed from Catholic to Protestant. A new pattern for worship was laid out in the Book of Common Prayer, largely written by Cranmer, which was to bring a sense of uniformity to the churches across England.

However, when Edward fell ill and died, his half-sister, Mary I (1516-1558)—a staunch Catholic—became queen. Because of her brutality and persecution of Protestants, overseeing the execution of over 280 Protestants (including Thomas Cranmer) she has become known as "Bloody Mary."

Understandably, many Protestants fled for safety to the Continent. They ended up in bastions of Reformation thought and practice, like Strasbourg and Geneva, which proved to be important for the development of Reformation ideas back in England. When Mary died in 1558 and her Protestant half-sister, Elizabeth, took the throne, these exiles returned to England with a greater zeal to see a more complete and thorough Reformation take place in England.

The Puritans

Unfortunately, Elizabeth I (1533-1603) adopted a politically wise agenda—known as the *via media*, the "middle way"—between a Protestant theology and a Roman Catholic look. While the theology changed back to Protestantism, the structure and feel of worship still looked like Roman Catholicism. Elizabeth also changed her title from Supreme Head of the Church of England to "Supreme Governor" (as Jesus is the only "Head" of the church).

Many, however, were not happy with this middle-road and wanted to purify the Church of England from its Roman Catholic vestiges. These became known as the "*Puritans*."

But while there were many varieties of Puritans, a Puritan was one who reacted against Elizabeth's *via media* in favor of a more thorough reformation in England; one who promoted evangelism, catechism (a series of questions and answers), and spiritual growth through the preaching and teaching of the Bible; one who embraced the doctrines of justification by faith alone and God's saving work by grace alone; and one who strove for personal holiness.

In particular, the Puritans—or as one historian called them, "intense Protestants"— wanted to purify the Church of England from certain practices and symbols: ministers wearing ceremonial vestments and surplices (religious clothing) that symbolized a mediatorial role between God and man. The Puritans rightly believed that Jesus was the *only* Mediator between God and man (cf. 1 Tim. 2:5). They wanted to remove crucifixes (crosses with Jesus on them) because Christ had risen from the dead. They sought to eliminate kneeling at Communion because it was seen as worshiping the bread and wine, which is idolatry. The Puritans wanted more preaching, catechism, and church discipline against immoral parishioners and clergy. To some, they seemed like killjoys and, thus, their neighbors did not always like them!

When Elizabeth died in 1603, James VI of Scotland became James I of England, uniting the two kingdoms under one monarch. James had a Protestant upbringing, which gave false hope (as it turned out) to the Puritans. Even though the Puritans argued their case before him—against the bishops at the Hampton Court Conference in 1604—James sided with the bishops and the establishment, who said, "No bishop, no king." James believed that his monarchy and the church government stood or fell together. Thus, the Catholic structure, its look and feel remained bonded to a Protestant theology. This is seen today in the Anglican and Episcopal Churches.

However, not all was lost. James did order a fresh translation of the Bible, published in 1611, as the "King James" (KJV) or "Authorized Version"—the most influential Bible ever produced in the English-speaking world. James also required all churches to subscribe to the Book of Common Prayer, but he didn't do a great job at *enforcing* his policies against the Puritans. His successor, however, King Charles I, did enforce policy and many Puritans came under intense persecution for not conforming to the state church.

The Scottish Reformation

We should note, at this point, that Scotland went through a more thorough Reformation more rapidly. In 1547, when England was about to convert to Protestantism, Scotland was still controlled by the Catholic French. However, St. Andrews was a Protestant holdout and a young fiery man named John Knox (1514-1572) tutored there. The French stormed the city and took Knox prisoner to serve on a big rowboat called a galley.

After two years, in 1549, he was released and took refuge in England. However, when "Bloody Mary" took the throne in 1553, he fled to Geneva, where he met Calvin. In a letter in 1556, Knox stated that Geneva "is the most perfect school of Christ that ever was in the earth since the days of the apostles." He stayed busy in Geneva, preaching several times a week and conducting multiple meetings and visitations.

In a rather unfortunate set of circumstances, Knox wrote a pamphlet entitled *The First Blast of the Trumpet Against the Monstrous Regiment of Women,* in which he attacked the idea that women (especially wicked women) should rule as queens. He called them "harlots," "monsters of nature," and "Jezebels." His antagonist, of course, was Queen Mary, but it was published the year that Mary died and Queen Elizabeth I took the throne (1558)—and Elizabeth was quite offended! In fact, she never forgave him and refused to let Knox back into England for the rest of his life!

Thus, Knox travelled straight to his homeland in Scotland in 1559. Upon arrival, Knox pushed through a series of Protestant reformations, leading to a formal break with the Roman Catholic Church the next year. The Church of Scotland also produced the Scots Confession of Faith—largely the work of Knox—which expressed the theology of Calvin. Knox continued to encourage a thorough reformation in Scotland, ministering in

Edinburgh at St. Giles Cathedral until his death in 1572.

War and Westminster

As mentioned earlier, Charles I set out to enforce his anti-Puritan policies when he took the throne in 1625. He demanded absolute conformity to the use of the Book of Common Prayer and the ceremonies that many Protestants couldn't stand. In 1638, Charles also tried to force these policies on the Scots, who were by that time fully Presbyterian and not under the control of the Church of England. Bad move!

The Scots rebelled. One lady, Jenny Geddes, reportedly threw a stool at the minister in St. Giles who started using the Book of Common Prayer in the worship service! Charles was furious at the Scots' response and sent an army up to squelch the rebellion. But to his great consternation, the Scots beat his army and the English were forced to retreat. Charles went to Parliament to ask for more money to fight the Scots only to be handed what was called the "Grand Remonstrance of 1640," which stipulated that they would grant Charles the money *only if* he agreed to their list of grievances; particularly, (1) that only Parliament can raise taxes and not the king and (2) that he must stop the oppression of religious uniformity.

Being an arrogant individual Charles took this as a direct assault to his kingship and declared war on his own Parliament! From 1642 to 1648, England was torn in a brutal Civil War. The two armies fought back and forth with Parliament finally coming out on top, thanks to the Scots coming alongside them to fight and the brilliant English leaders, Oliver Cromwell (1599-1658) and General Thomas Fairfax (1612-1671). King Charles was captured, brought up on charges, and beheaded on January 30, 1649.

Significantly, throughout the war, Parliament controlled the southeastern portion of England, including London. It was there, at Westminster Abbey, that a gathering of nearly 130 ministers would meet from 1643 to 1647 to write one of the most beloved and influential confessions of faith, the *Westminster Confession of Faith*. They also composed a Larger and Shorter Catechism and a Directory for Public Worship.

With Charles executed, England was declared a republic and quickly chose Oliver Cromwell to be their leader. Refusing the title of "king," Cromwell became "Lord Protector of the Commonwealth of England." Many attribute the 1650s to be the *triumph* of Puritanism. In reality, the sudden change to a Commonwealth caused irreparable damage to the Puritan cause. Disorder, chaos, and confusion reigned and, after only a decade, the people wanted a return to the monarchy.

The Great Persecution

By 1660, the pendulum of national favor swung back toward a monarchy and Charles II (Charles I's son) was crowned king—bringing with him the Restoration of the Church of England and the persecution of the Puritans. This period became hauntingly known as the *Great Persecution*. Many faced torture, fines, imprisonment, loss of civil liberties, denial of access to the universities, and (in some cases) execution; all this for simply not conforming to the official church.

After Charles II's arrival, thirteen men involved in the execution of his father were themselves executed for treason. Two years later, in 1662, Charles enacted the *Act of Uniformity*, demanding that all ministers and churches be uniform, prescribing to the worship as outlined in the Book of Common Prayer. That August, nearly 2,000 ministers, professors, and church leaders (called "nonconformists" or "dissenters") conscientiously objected and were, thereby, forced out! In 1665, these dissenters were evicted from five miles from their town of ministry—known as the Five Mile Act.

One of these dissenters, John Flavel (c.1630-1691) suffered continual persecution from state officials while trying to lead his congregation in the city of Dartmouth. He also suffered grief from the loss of three wives, a son, and his parents who died from being incarcerated for holding a "nonconformist" worship service. However, being forced from his town of ministry afforded Flavel (like many other Puritans) time to write. This is one of the reasons why we have so much Puritan literature from the later 17th century!

Another one of these dissenters, John Bunyan (1628-1688), was confined to the Bedford jail for over twelve years of his life, preaching in secret and often barely avoiding execution.[1] While there—making shoelaces for a wage—he began to write what would become one of the greatest pieces of literature, *The Pilgrim's Progress.* No other book in English, except the Bible, has been so widely read over such a long period. First published in 1678, it has never been out of print and has been translated into over 200 languages!

After Charles II died in 1685, his brother James II took the throne. James was a Roman Catholic and the nation erupted in protest— many out of fear—at a Catholic sitting on the throne. After only three years, James was forced out with the peaceful "invasion"

---

[1] For an overview of Bunyan's life, see Brian H. Cosby, *John Bunyan: The Journey of a Pilgrim* (Ross-Shire, Scotland: Christian Focus Publications, 2009).

of William and Mary, an event known as the Glorious Revolution. In 1689, they enacted the Act of Toleration, which finally granted religious freedom to the Puritans.

During the 16th and 17th centuries, England witnessed a turbulent Reformation and *Post*-Reformation, as the nation tried to implement the new changes of theology and worship into their everyday lives. Through war, persecution, and triumph, England—which began as a decisively Roman Catholic nation—had become a decisively Protestant nation. This had a profound impact on the establishment of the New World.

DISCUSSION QUESTIONS

- How did the Church of England officially begin? Did Henry VIII really like Protestant (Reformed) theology?
- If someone were to ask you, "Who was a Puritan?" what would you say? What's the first thought that comes to your head when you think of a "Puritan"?
- Many Puritans spent time in jail for their faith. What would happen if the nation you lived in suddenly turned strongly against the Christian faith and put Christians in prison? How would you react?

ENLIGHTENMENT AND AWAKENING (A.D. 1700-1800)

Like most teenagers I know, I've struggled with early mornings. As I passed through my 20s and now into my 30s, I'm *still* not a morning person. But the dark colored, rich tasting, simmering hot, earthy smell of coffee in the morning awakens me to realize that coffee is a wonderful proof that God loves us. At least, that's my take on it! Being energized after feeling lifeless has also been witnessed in the church at various times through its history. But spiritual vitality usually falls on the heels of lukewarm lethargy.

In 1620 one hundred Separatists—those wanting to leave England mainly because of religious persecution—left for the New World on the *Mayflower* and landed in Massachusetts (they had intended on landing further south in Virginia). They quickly set up civil laws that required a close connection with God's laws, to the point that only those converted to Christianity were allowed to vote!

Several prominent people had qualms about this, including the Baptist Separatist, Roger Williams (1603-1683), who objected to the idea of civil judges enforcing religious beliefs. In 1635, they banished Williams from the colony and he travelled southwest to a little bay, which he bought from some local Native Americans and called it "Providence." He declared that no person would be called into question regarding matters of religion—welcoming any and all—and established the first Baptist Church in America. Williams would later welcome the exiled spiritualist, Anne Hutchinson, to Providence. These little ideas of religious liberty and the separation of church and state would change the world and set the agenda for the American spirit.

In Europe, people began rejecting the older institutional religion of their forefathers; some rejected certain core doctrines of the Christian faith while others pulled away from the faith altogether. Still others rejected the older forms of church government and embraced an individual spiritual experience with God apart from the institution of the church. However the pieces fell, one thing was clear: people questioned and rejected the institutional Christianity of the past.

Enlightenment and Deism

One of these movements began during the later 1600s, when many began insisting that truth could be obtained simply through reason, observation, and experiment. By arriving at "truth" from this angle, they argued, differing religions and world-views should tolerate one another though all should reject the mystical and superstitious elements of religious faith. This movement eventually mushroomed in the 1700s into what we now call the *Enlightenment*.

One of the principal early movers of the Enlightenment was Isaac Newton (1642-1727), the English physicist and mathematician who sought to explain the observable universe *not* through the lens of the Bible, but through science and math— especially through the laws of motion and gravity. At one point, Newton said, "Gravity explains the motions of the planets, but it cannot explain who set the planets in motion."

Newton, who considered himself a "Christian" and yet rejected the doctrine of the Trinity, added fuel to the growing belief of his time, *Deism*. Deism is a system of natural religion that sees God as the first Cause (or first Mover), the being who set the solar system in motion under a variety of secondary laws and then sits back to let it be governed on its own *by* those laws. In other words, God was seen as the great Clock-Maker who created all things (wound up the clock) and then let it go. Thus, deists reject miracles, divine providence, and God's continuing involvement in the world (ironically, though they reject miracles, they affirm the "miracle" of creation!).

Pietism

But not everybody was abandoning the faith and explaining the world through purely secular means. Some, like the *Pietists*, moved in the opposite direction of the Deists toward a deeply spiritual expression of the Christian faith. A German named Philipp Jakob Spener (1635-1705)—who had been influenced by the writings of the Reformers and the Puritans—witnessed the spiritual decline of the Lutheran church into a state of apathy.

Wanting to revive the sterile spiritual condition of the people, Spener began hosting devotional meetings in his house twice a week, which he called *Collegia Pietatis* ("schools of piety"). During that time, he also wrote *Pia Desideria* (1675), which sought to supplant the emphasis on the institution of the church with an emphasis on personal piety and spirituality. His followers soon became known as the Pietists and, while they wanted to see and experience greater zeal for God within the church, many didn't want to simply form a new church or separate from Lutheranism.

In the early stages, Pietism was underfunded and didn't gain much traction until the contribution of the wealthy Count, Nicolaus Zinzendorf (1700-1760). Spener had a profound effect upon the young Zinzendorf, even becoming the latter's godfather! Moreover, Zinzendorf attended Halle University, a Pietist stronghold, and later settled down on a large estate and began printing inexpensive Bibles, catechisms, hymnals, and various Christian books. Like Spener, Zinzendorf wanted to revive the "dead" (as he saw it) Christianity in Europe.

In 1722, Protestant immigrants (many from Moravia) who also supported the spiritual emphasis of Pietism began showing up at his door asking for asylum and assistance. He welcomed them with open arms, allowing them to take up residence on his expansive estate. As time went on and more immigrants flooded his estate, he began devoting himself to their spiritual care.

They set up their own town, called Herrnhut, a few miles away, and became known as the Moravian Brethren. However, due to their emphasis on personal piety over and against the hierarchy of the church, Zinzendorf and many of Herrnhut's leaders were exiled. Zinzendorf soon established Pietist communities all over, notably in the Netherlands, England, the West Indies, South Africa, and North America.

John Wesley and the Methodists

The Moravian message eventually reached the ears of a young minister in the Church of England, John Wesley (1703-1791). While at Oxford University, Wesley and his brother Charles (the great hymn writer) started the "Holy Club," which strove to attain a holy lifestyle through various *methods*, including Bible reading, prayer, fasting, personal examination, and meeting together. Over time, their fellow students began calling them *Methodists* who derided their methodical structure of the Christian life.

In 1735, after his time at Oxford, John sailed for Savannah, Georgia, to be the minister of the newly formed church there. At one point on the voyage, a violent storm came upon them. The crew and its travellers feared for their lives, except for a small group of Moravian Brethren who joyfully sang psalms and prayed. Wesley immediately knew they possessed a spirituality that he lacked.

After Wesley's disastrous experience in Georgia, he returned to England and joined a Moravian community. One day, while walking outside of a Moravian meeting on Aldersgate Street in London, he overheard the reading of one of Martin Luther's sermons on the book of Romans. Wesley, recognizing both his sin and God's grace, was saved! He later recounted of that event, "I felt my heart strangely warmed."

Because of Wesley's involvement with the Moravians, he was banned from preaching in the Church of England. Thus, he decided to join his friend and former Holy Club member, George Whitefield (1714-1770), who had been preaching out in the open air. For the next fifty years, Wesley became known for his open-air preaching in fields, cottages, and chapels. Over time, he also organized his followers in the Methodist Society in England.

Like the Pietists in Germany, Wesley and his Methodists wanted to bring spiritual revival to the Church of England. However, it soon became clear that his vision would not be realized and so the Methodists became organized into a separate structure and denomination, the Methodist Church. Wesley briefly parted ways with Whitefield in 1741 over the doctrine of predestination as Wesley was Arminian and Whitefield affirmed the doctrines of grace from the Reformation. While the two never agreed on this issue, they reunited and remained friends for the rest of their lives.

The Great Awakening

George Whitefield, himself aligned with the Calvinistic strand of Methodism, also had interests in Georgia where he set up a well-known orphanage. But Whitefield soon became known for much more than his care for orphans; his preaching up and down the eastern coast of New England would spark the *Great Awakening.*

The Great Awakening was a widespread revival during the 1730s and 40s, but reached its peak in New England during that time. Those who heard Whitefield— known for his ability to project his voice to thousands—often became deeply aware of their own personal need for salvation in Christ. His preaching circuit during 1739 and 1740 catapulted him to celebrity status, even winning the applause of notables such as Benjamin Franklin (though Franklin rejected Whitefield's theology). But while the rumblings of revival were beginning to shake the American colonies, it was not until the rather dispassionate preaching of one New Englander that the true zenith of the

Great Awakening began. That preacher was Jonathan Edwards (1703-1758).

As early as 1734, Edwards witnessed some early revivals in his church in Northampton, Massachusetts. Edwards' sermons usually lasted upwards of two hours with him simply reading his manuscript in a monotone voice. But the Spirit of God attended the Word of God as it was preached and revival broke out in the Northampton church. Hundreds came to saving faith in Christ and parishioners became passionately and emotionally involved in their affections for God and his Word. Soon, the contagious spirit of revival spread and New England became caught up in the Awakening.

Not all, of course, were thrilled with the new enthusiasm, as many of the revivalists disparaged church authority and institutionalism. Soon, a split occurred between the Old Lights (the traditionalists) and the New Lights (those in favor of the Awakening).

Edwards would go on to become America's most significant and original philosophical theologian. A strong Calvinist and supporter of the Awakening, Edwards preached the famous sermon, "Sinners in the Hands of an Angry God," and he authored a number of books, including *Freedom of the Will* (1754),

A Treatise Concerning Religious Affections (1746), and his most popular, *The Life and Diary of David Brainerd, Missionary to the Indians* (1749).

Brainerd and the Native Americans

In 1748, David Brainerd (1718-1747) a twenty-nine-year-old missionary to the Native Americans died in the home of Jonathan Edwards.[1] Edwards took the young man's diary, edited it, and published it the next year, originally titled *An Account of the Life of the Late Rev. David Brainerd.* It would be Edwards' most frequently reprinted work—having never been out of print since—and influenced the later missionary endeavors of William Carey (1761-1834) and Jim Elliot (1927–1956).

Organized missions to the American Indians had initially taken shape under the ministry of the Puritan John Eliot (1604-1690), often referred to as "the apostle to the Indians." The early American colonials had regular (and sometimes hostile!) engagement with the Native Americans throughout the 17th century, especially as they expanded westward into Indian territory. Eliot's missions focused on the Massachusetts Indians and even translated the Bible into their language in 1663.

[1] For an overview of Brainerd's life, see Brian H. Cosby, *David Brainerd: A Love for the Lost* (Ross-Shire, Scotland: Christian Focus Publications, 2011).

By the early 1700s, a number of Christian societies had been set up in England, Scotland, and New England for the purpose of reaching the Indians. After being licensed to preach by some "New Light" ministers, David Brainerd benefited from and was approved by the Scottish Society for Promoting Christian Knowledge (SSPCK) for this purpose. After Brainerd was unduly expelled from Yale for a disparaging remark about a teacher, he embarked on a number of exhausting and unrelenting missions to the Indians in New York, Pennsylvania, Massachusetts, and New Jersey. All said, Brainerd travelled over 3,000 miles on horseback and continually suffered from chronic illness, fatigue, and the harsh conditions of frontier life. He died from tuberculosis in Edwards' home at the young age of twenty-nine. Brainerd's life and ill treatment by the authorities at Yale also inspired the beginnings of a new college, the College of New Jersey (later renamed Princeton University).

While the Great Awakening sparked revival among the American colonies during the 1740s, religious zeal slowly disappeared toward the end of the 18th century. By the 1780s, less than thirty per cent of the population in America held membership in a local church. Moreover, the American Revolution and subsequent split from

England also split churches and Christian communions. Anglicans in America became the Protestant Episcopal Church while Deism remained alive and well during the formation of the new American Constitution and society. Confusion and disunity together launched England and New England Christianity into the 19th century.

DISCUSSION QUESTIONS

- The pilgrims coming to the new world had a unique opportunity. But imagine if you could set up a new society and establish any system of government and religion you chose to set up, what would it look like? Why?

- John Wesley and his "Holy Club" sought to practice a life of holiness? What is the role of the Holy Spirit?

- It has been common to see Christians schedule a "revival" at their church. What are your thoughts about this practice? Who causes a revival to take place?

- Can you think of some difficulties and hardships faced by the early American settlers? Do you think you could not only survive, but thrive and enjoy life back then under those conditions?

ABANDONING THE BIBLE
(A.D. 1800-1900)

It's easy to get lost if you don't have a map, or it's raining at night and you don't have a torch. It's also easy to get lost if you don't have the sure rule and guide of faith, the Word of God. But that's exactly what happened during the 19th century.

The 19th century witnessed a cultural break from historic Christian theology, prominence, and worship. The emphasis on human reason—triumphing during the 18th century—together with the scientific and industrial revolutions during the 19th century, created the platform for the population centers of Europe and America to move away from evangelical Protestant Christianity. This departure may be summarized by the *abandonment* of biblical doctrine and piety in favor of (1) extra-biblical revivalism, (2) liberalism, (3) cults, and (4) evolution.

Abandonment 1: Revivalism

By the beginning of 1800, Christians began opposing the onslaught of Deism and secular humanism, eventually sparking what has been called the *Second Great Awakening* during the early 1800s. A central belief was the return of Christ after the millennial (one-thousand year) reign of Christ (cf. Rev. 20). This *Postmillennialism*, as it came to be called, taught that it was every Christian's duty to transform and purify society in preparation for Christ's return. This effort, of course, fell into a state of disillusionment with the arrival of an even greater abandonment of biblical Christianity.

The Second Great Awakening also coincided with other new forms of Christian practice during the early 1800s. One was the birth of modern *revivalism*, thanks to the efforts of the young American evangelist Charles Finney (1792-1875). Originally a Presbyterian, Finney abandoned historic Reformed forms of Christian practice and worship and set up camp meetings or "tent revivals."

During these meetings, Finney introduced a number of religious practices that later became galvanized in the culture of American Christianity, which were called Finney's "new measures": the anxious bench,[1] having

---

[1] The "anxious bench" was a bench or a series of seats near the pulpit at revivals reserved for those who were especially concerned about their spiritual condition. These concerned individuals were expected to sit near the front for special prayer and attention by the preacher or spiritual leaders.

women pray in public meetings, unrehearsed and dramatized preaching, and an early form of the "altar call." Many times, local shops and businesses would close down when Finney came to town as his meetings would oftentimes last several days on end, drawing huge crowds.

On the back of these new religious inventions of Finney was the belief that humans didn't have a sinful nature, but a nature that was functionally neutral and therefore could be simply persuaded by human reason and emotional charge to "accept" Jesus. Unlike Jonathan Edwards, who almost a century earlier attributed the First Great Awakening to the supernatural and sovereign work of God, Finney attributed the Awakenings of his day to mere human engineering. Thus, Finney contributed to the growing "New Side" movement that rejected the historic Protestant and Reformed forms of the Christian faith.

Other developments, like the advent of Sunday School in England by Robert Raikes (1736-1811), which quickly invaded the churches in the United States and the growing call for the abolition of slavery in America (following England's lead) had enormous effects for the churches in the West. The former introduced age-segregated instruction in the church and the decline of *parental* involvement in the religious education of their children while the latter split the United States, North and South, along with its churches.

Along with the growing revivalism came a new wave of interpreting the Bible: *Dispensationalism*. Made popular by the writings of John Nelson Darby (1800-1882), Dispensationalism taught that God's work was divided into seven distinct eras (or "dispensations") throughout redemptive history, which stood opposed to the covenantal theology from the Reformation. Most Dispensationalists believe that Christians will be taken from the earth before the final judgment, Christ's establishment of a literal one thousand-year reign, and that the nation of Israel will play a significant role in the end-times events. Dispensationalism became a widespread belief, thanks to the efforts of the *Scofield Reference Bible*, Lewis Sperry Chafer, Charles Ryrie, Dwight Pentecost, Dallas Theological Seminary, and the bestselling series by Tim LaHaye and Jerry Jenkins, *Left Behind*.

Abandonment 2: Liberalism

While the United States spiraled into a bloody Civil War during the early 1860s over states rights, money, and slavery, another anti-Christian movement rose in prominence on the Continent of Europe: *liberal theology*.

Indeed, the starting ground of liberal theology is a rejection of the Bible *as* the Word of God and a disregard for its inerrant, infallible, and inspired characteristics. Therefore, the Scriptures are not seen as factual, historical, and accurate writings, but rather poetic, purely human accounts of people and events.

Liberal theology rode the coat tails of the Enlightenment and the rejection of the supernatural. But, in opposition to the Enlightenment, liberal theology highlighted emotion and feeling as the dominant force of religion. Most liberal scholars denied the miraculous and supernatural events as recorded in the Bible, such as the Virgin Birth of Christ, Jesus' healing miracles, the sacrificial atonement of Christ on the cross, and his resurrection.

It began in German higher education (colleges and seminaries) in the early 19th century and grew into an international standard of biblical and theological studies by the early 20th century. Chief among its architects was the German theologian, Friedrich Schleiermacher (1768-1834), known as the "Father of Modern Liberal Theology."

Schleiermacher emphasized *feeling* as the basis of religion and that all religions— all "valid" and true—experience a feeling of dependence upon the infinite through different expressions, albeit Christianity is the "highest" expression. All that truly mattered, he taught, was what Jesus said about divine love and social justice. His theology was subjective, not basing his ideas upon the concrete objective realities found in Scripture. A long line of liberal theologians has since adorned Schleiermacher's thought: Henry Ward Beecher, Adolf von Harnack, Albrecht Ritschl, Harry Emerson Fosdick, Rudolf Bultmann, Paul Tillich, John Hick, and John Shelby Spong.

Ironically, during the 20th century, despite the efforts of liberal theologians to be more "tolerant" and "accepting" of all religions (except for conservative Christianity!), liberal denominations of all stripes decreased in membership by *seventy per cent* from 1930 to 2000. Conforming *to* the world was blending in *with* the world, which had the effect of losing its distinction *from* the world. This is not the faith passed down from the apostles and prophets.

Abandonment 3: Cults

A third type of abandonment from historic, biblical Christianity during the 19th century was the advent of various cults, especially *Mormonism* and *Jehovah's Witnesses*. Both are modern-day heresies that have clouded biblical doctrine and are often taught and viewed under the guise of "Christianity."

Mormonism—also called the "Church of Jesus Christ of Latter-Day Saints"—began in 1830 when the twenty-four-year-old Joseph Smith (1805-1844) from New York claimed to have received divine revelation on golden tablets, which he recorded as *The Book of Mormon* (these tablets, of course, are nowhere to be found). Mormons teach that after Christ's resurrection, he visited the Americas and that one day the new Zion will be established in the Western hemisphere. They also believe that Jesus is at war with his brother, Satan, and Jesus is *not* God (remember the Arians?). In fact, Joseph Smith's own edition of the Bible, which he largely made up, re-translates various passages to reflect the non-deity of Jesus. For example, his edition of the Gospel of John, Chapter 1, begins: "In the beginning was the gospel preached through the Son. And the gospel was the word, and the word was with the Son, and the Son was with God, and the Son was of God." This, as you are probably aware, is very different from what John 1 actually states.

In 1843, Smith had another revelation in which he was told that polygamy (having multiple spouses) was to be an "everlasting covenant" and, therefore, was sanctioned by God. Several years later, in 1847, his successor, Brigham Young, moved the Mormon headquarters to Salt Lake City, Utah, where they remain to this day. Additionally, Mormons have developed a number of other extra-biblical practices such as the wearing of "holy underwear" and performing marriages and baptisms for the dead.

Like Mormonism, Jehovah's Witnesses (JW) deny the historic doctrine of the Trinity. Jesus, they contend, is not God. And, like Mormons, they too have their own "translation" of the Bible, which obviously doesn't come from the original Greek and Hebrew languages.

JW began in the 1870s under the teachings of Charles Taze Russell (1852-1916), who led the Bible Student movement in Pittsburg, Pennsylvania. Russell taught that Christ had invisibly returned to earth in 1874 to prepare for the Kingdom of God which was expected to come to full fruition in 1914. The group's original name—the Watch Tower Tract and Bible Society—changed to Jehovah's Witnesses in 1931. Russell's publication, *Zion's Watchtower and Herald of Christ's Presence*, changed to what is now called *The Watchtower* and is currently the most widely circulated magazine in the world (nearly 45 million copies per month). JW are well known for refusing to honor symbols of national identity (flags, pledge of allegiance, etc.), their refusal of participating in blood transfusions, their refusal of military service, and their door-to-door evangelizing.

Abandonment 4: Evolution

While extra-biblical revivalism, liberal theology, and various cults all demonstrated an abandonment of the Bible, *the* dominant force that would shape and has continued to shape the worldview of Christian and non-Christian alike in the Western world was the advent of anti-Christian, evolutionary theory—thanks in part to the watershed book by Charles Darwin (1809-1882), *The Origin of Species* (1859). Remarkably, by the 1870s, most of the scientific community and the general public accepted evolution as fact. For his part, Darwin didn't invent evolution, but simply caught the mood of his time, added "evidence," and made it popular.

Generally, the term "evolution" refers to the belief that all animals (humans included) have descended from one common ancestor. How? Evolutionists argue that rain fell upon the rocks of the earth billions of years ago (the numbers keep changing), and then the subsequent primordial goo somehow came alive (though nobody knows how). All of a sudden, the simple cell (which is actually incredibly complex) formed on its own and then—through a series of mutations and the process of the "survival of the fittest"—we get the plethora of species, plants, wildlife, animals, and humans that we see today.

Simply put, evolutionary theory was meant to explain all that we see and observe *apart* from the supernatural creation of God as it is revealed in the Bible. Interestingly, "science," technically speaking, refers to that which can be observed, tested, and repeated. *Evolution from one species to another (a dog to a non-dog, ape to human, etc.) has never been observed.* Thus, evolution is technically not science and it certainly hasn't been proven.

The fact of the matter is that evolution takes a great deal of faith. Not only does it go against the clear teachings of Scripture, it is not supported by unbiased scientific fact. Nevertheless, Darwin's thought has infiltrated every aspect of society—from schools to Sunday schools, government policy to environmentalism and it was set up as an entire worldview in opposition to the Christian faith.

Light in the Darkness

Despite the overarching abandonment of the Bible during the 19th century, there was some light in the darkness. Notable theologians like the Princetonians, Charles Hodge (1797-1878) and Benjamin B. Warfield (1851-1921), and preachers such as Charles Spurgeon

(1834-1892), J. C. Ryle (1816-1900), and Robert Murray McCheyne (1813-1843) continued to champion the historic Protestant faith. God always preserves a remnant and he continually supplies his church with able minsters, teachers, and shepherds.

Extra-biblical revivalism, liberal theology, cults, and the theory of evolution converged to make the 19th century a period of time of the *abandonment* of the Bible for a large segment of once-professing "Christians." Together, they mark a decisive break with the historic, Protestant, and biblical faith of previous generations.

DISCUSSION QUESTIONS

- Give a summary statement of each of the four "abandonments" as surveyed in this chapter.
- Many today try to predict when Jesus will return. Do you think this is biblical? Why or why not?
- It was noted that "liberal" churches are declining in membership at a rapid rate. Why do you think this is happening?
- Were you taught evolution in school? There remains to this day no documented scientific observation of evolution (e.g. a dog to a non-dog). Why, then, do you think it is so emphasized by academic institutions?

FUNDAMENTALISM, EVANGELICALISM, AND GLOBAL CHRISTIANITY (A.D. 1900-PRESENT)

Liberalism and evolutionary theory didn't have the last say. Christians from a variety of backgrounds and denominations rallied to the *fundamentals* of the faith while others directly addressed the theological fallacies of liberal theology. Still others, seeking to re-establish a first century expression of Christianity, sought to engage the "signs and wonders" (healings, speaking in tongues, etc.) as seen in the Bible. The message from all of these was clear: historic Christianity was far from over.

All of these were reactions to the offspring of the Enlightenment, which include liberal theology, evolutionary theory, Deism, cults, and the "scientific/modernism" revolution. Those reacting to these various heresies and unbiblical propositions eventually merged into the movement now known as *evangelicalism.* Today, evangelicalism— despite its manifold stripes and diversity— generally holds to conservative, historic, orthodox, and biblical doctrines. Strikingly, while the evangelical movement is shrinking in America and Europe, it is exploding in Africa, Asia, and South America.

Fundamentalism

Two men, A. C. Dixon and Reuben Archer Torrey, edited and released twelve volumes entitled *The Fundamentals* between 1910 and 1915, which sought to explain the "non-negotiables" of the Christian faith. They defended orthodox Protestant Reformed Christianity against liberalism, Catholicism, Mormonism, atheism, and (to some degree) evolution. *The Fundamentals* sparked a movement, joined by the rank and file of conservative Protestants of all denominations (especially Baptists and Presbyterians) in the United States and, to a lesser extent, Europe.

As the first title was being released in 1910, the Presbyterian Church in the USA declared that there were "five fundamentals" that were necessary and essential to the Christian faith: (1) inspiration and inerrancy of the Bible, (2) the virgin birth of Jesus, (3) the substitutionary atonement of Christ on the cross, (4) the bodily resurrection of Christ from the dead, and (5) the historical reality of Jesus' miracles. These five fundamentals became a test of Christian orthodoxy for ministers.

Fourteen years later, these five fundamentals were directly attacked in the "Auburn Affirmation" of 1924 (from Auburn, New York and Auburn Theological Seminary), which garnered more than 1,200 signatures from church leaders and ably expressed the growing division within the church—what is now called the "Fundamentalist-Modernist Controversy."

Fundamentalism, broadly speaking, also found expression in a small-town courthouse in Dayton, Tennessee during the blistering-hot summer of 1925—at the *Scopes "Monkey" Trial.* John Scopes, a high school science teacher, taught evolution in the public school, which violated Tennessee's Butler Act. The American Civil Liberties Union (ACLU) decided to fund the defense—led by the famous defense attorney Clarence Darrow—while the three-time US presidential nominee, William Jennings Bryan, represented the prosecution. In this high-profile, highly-publicized trial, the issue over evolution and creation in government education became an expression of the undercurrents of division within the United States between fundamentalism and modernism.

Interestingly, at the heart of the Scopes trail was the *Civic Biology* textbook by George Hunter (published in 1914) used by Scopes, which affirmed the following:

The Races of Man. At the present time there exist upon the earth five races or varieties of man, each very different from the other in instincts, social customs, and, to an extent, in structure. These are the Ethiopian or negro type, originating in Africa; the Malay or brown race, from the islands of the Pacific; the American Indian; the Mongolian or yellow race, including the natives of China, Japan, and the Eskimos; and finally, the highest type of all, the Caucasians, represented by the civilized white inhabitants of Europe and America.

This racism isn't too dissimilar to the subtitle from Charles Darwin's famous book, the full title being: *The Origin of Species by Means of Natural Selection; or, the Preservation of Favoured Races in the Struggle for Life.* Evolution is, from its foundation, racist.

Neo-orthodoxy

Another response to the modern and liberal theology movement of the 19th century was *Neo-orthodoxy*, its chief proponents being Karl Barth (1886-1968) and Emil Brunner (1899-1966), even though they weren't too fond of the label and they sometimes differed on each other's particular theological issues.

Neo-orthodoxy revived various themes of Reformed theology that had been snubbed by liberal theology (i.e. the sovereignty of God, human sinfulness, etc.). Theology, Barth and Brunner taught, was to be founded upon the Bible (though they didn't believe it to be inerrant). The Bible is God's revelation to humanity; religion, on the other hand, is man's attempt to grasp God. Thus, one cannot attain to a right understanding of God simply through observing nature. They also stressed the absolute transcendence of God; that God is wholly independent of the material universe—the "wholly *Other*." Though erroneous at places and left unfinished, some have argued that Barth's *Church Dogmatics* remains the most detailed and extensive expression of Protestant doctrine since the time of the Reformation.

Pentecostalism

A third reaction to the rise of modernism was *Pentecostalism*. Remember John Wesley? Wesley believed, among other things, that a Christian could actually become holy or sanctified in this life. During the 19th century, the *Holiness movement*—as it came to be known as—borrowed Wesley's theology and promoted it, affirming instantaneous sanctification.

Though started in the Methodist Church (which Wesley founded), bishops during the later 19th century started to separate themselves from the Holiness movement. The withdrawing Holiness groups from the Methodist Church emphasized "alter calls," invitations, testimonies, decisions for Christ, and other revivalist-leaning techniques. Physical healings and speaking in tongues would also become associated with the Holiness movement.

Then, in 1906, an event would break the mold. William J. Seymour, an African-American son of former slaves, began preaching in a small house in Los Angeles concerning the baptism of the Holy Spirit and why speaking in tongues accompanied true conversion. After the house became no longer adequate to accommodate the large crowds, an old mission on Azusa Street was purchased. Immediately, revival broke out. Thousands filled the mission and surrounding areas and the three-year Azusa Street Revival became the birthplace of the modern Pentecostal movement.

Most Pentecostals believe that one can receive the same experience and spiritual gifts, as did the first Christians on the day of Pentecost (Acts 2). Pentecostals also emphasize personal power granted by the Holy Spirit to overcome hardship and a large segment believe in the heretical "*health, wealth, and prosperity gospel,*" which teaches that if you are faithful enough, God will give you health, wealth, and financial prosperity.

While there remains no central governing branch or authority within Pentecostalism, it is one of the fastest-growing movements in the world, particularly in the global south. Some well-known leaders of the Pentecostal and charismatic movement include Oral Roberts, Benny Hinn, Pat Robertson, Jimmy Swaggart, Kenneth Copeland, Kenneth Hagin, T. D. Jakes, Joyce Meyer, and Joel Osteen. Other popular charismatic groups— which often associate with Pentecostals—are the Hillsong Church (and Hillsong United band) in Australia and the Alpha Course, based out of Holy Trinity, Brompton, in London, England.

Evangelicalism

While "evangelicalism" can be traced to the Great Awakening in the 1730s and 1740s (see Chapter 9)—and theological and spiritual emphases before that from the Puritans— it broke away from the fundamentalism of the early 20th century into the movement as it is recognized today. Evangelicalism emphasizes the historically Protestant theological convictions—justification by faith alone, the substitutionary atonement of Christ on the cross, the miracles of Jesus, his resurrection, personal conversion and rebirth by the Spirit, the realities of heaven and hell, the sovereign grace of God, and the inspiration and authority of the Bible.

During the 1940s and especially in the 1950s—with the emergence of the evangelist Billy Graham (1918–) and his largely-popular crusades—evangelicalism began to differentiate itself from fundamentalism with fundamentalism focusing more on its distinction from liberalism while evangelicalism focused more on personal conversion experience, rebirth, assurance of salvation, and evangelism.

Evangelical zeal also permeated into the youth culture, as seen in the explosion of youth-oriented organizations like Young Life (1941), Youth for Christ (1946), Fellowship of Christian Athletes (1954), and Student Venture (1966). In response to the immediate popularity of these organizations and the supportive desire to see young people reached with the gospel, churches began their own version of "youth ministry." Youth ministry quickly became a church-norm, especially in the United States, even developing into its own culture with rock bands, skits, and inspirational talks by the newly-formed category—the Youth Pastor. Some today are calling for this culture of youth ministry to give up their gimmicks and return to a biblical model of means of grace ministry.

It should be noted, too, that other theologically conservative efforts sought to put a halt to the rise of liberal theology over the course of the 20th century in favor of a more evangelical and historic expression of faith. Earlier 20th century leaders included J. Gresham Machen, Martyn Lloyd-Jones, Francis Schaeffer, Carl Henry. More recently, champions of evangelical Christianity include John Stott, Abraham Kuyper, T. F. Torrance, J. I. Packer, R. C. Sproul, John MacArthur, John Piper, Timothy Keller, Rick Warren, and Albert Mohler.

Today, there are nearly 300 million evangelicals around the world from a diversity of backgrounds, denominations, and cultures. While the term "evangelical" is fairly loose in meaning, it represents a definite approach to historic, Bible-believing Christianity. In recent years, liberal spin-offs from evangelicalism have gained attention, such as postmodernism, the Emerging Church movement, and the acceptance of homosexuality in church leadership. Evangelicalism is currently in a state of transition and it yet remains clear as to its future development. All told, the 20th century witnessed the galvanization of both mainstream liberalism in the church as well as its reaction, expressed in fundamentalism, neo-orthodoxy, and recently, evangelicalism.

As we look back through the history of the Christian church, we see God's faithfulness to preserve his people in spite of their sin and rebellion against his truth. We see a great cloud of witnesses, generations of those who have embraced Christ by faith, beckoning us onward as we will one day be translated from the Church Militant to the Church Triumphant. And until that day comes, we pray, "Come quickly, Lord Jesus!"

DISCUSSION QUESTIONS

- Do you agree with the "five fundamentals" of the faith? Could you back them from Scripture?

- If you have simply evolved from some primordial goo, can there exist absolute morality? Can you have an ultimate right and wrong?

- What is the "health, wealth, and prosperity gospel"? Have you seen evidences on TV, the Internet, or in books?

- Who are some of the heroes of the faith for you? Why?

ABOUT THE AUTHOR

Brian H. Cosby (Ph.D., Australian College of Theology) is Pastor of Wayside Presbyterian Church (PCA) on Signal Mountain, Tennessee.

He is the author of a number of books, including *Giving Up Gimmicks: Reclaiming Youth Ministry from an Entertainment Culture*, *Rebels Rescued: A Student's Guide to Reformed Theology*, and two biographies in the Christian Focus Trailblazers Series, *John Bunyan: The Journey of a Pilgrim* and *David Brainerd: A Love for the Lost*.

Dietrich Bonhoeffer once said that between the Bible and us stands a church, a church with a history. We too often forget that, and such forgetfulness is not healthy for us. This book will help you remember. It will help you remember that we have a history, that our history matters, and that our history shapes who we are today. Brian Cosby has done you a huge favor. He's made reading church history easy and fun—and even devotional and worshipful. All you need to do is take up this book and read.

Stephen J. Nichols,
Research Professor of Christianity & Culture, Lancaster Bible College

Fast-paced and focused on major leaders and movements, this book gives a helpful introduction to the history of the church in bite-size portions. Throughout the ages, God's Story reminds us that it is His story—the account of God's works among His people.

Joel R. Beeke,
President of Puritan Reformed Theological Seminary,
Grand Rapids, Michigan

For those intimated by the broad sweep of church history—whether teenagers, college students, or adults—*God's Story* offers a breezy account of two thousand years in a format that would take only a couple of hours to read. But don't be fooled by the small package: here is robust, doxological history sure to offer wisdom to God's people and insight to the church's future leaders. Brian Cosby has done a favor for students everywhere, both young and old!

Sean Michael Lucas,
Senior Minister, First Presbyterian Church, Hattiesburg, Mississippi

God's Story by Dr. Brian Cosby will help students understand how the Church came into being, how she has developed and what she has taught in her history. I commend this book to you and pray high school and college students will pick it up in order to have an increasing passion to know and study the history of Christ's Church.

Dave Jenkins, Director, Servants of Grace Ministries

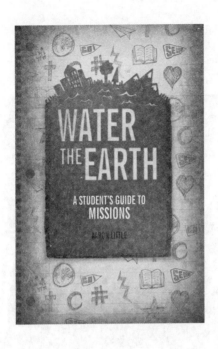

Water the Earth
A Student's Guide to Missions
by Aaron Little
ISBN: 978-1-78191-321-5

Look at mission from a perspective that will help you to understand your own mission, both life-long and short-term, and give you tips to accomplish outreach where you are called, whether around the world or down the street. Aaron Little reveals God's big-picture plan for missions while giving out handy details for your own evangelism in this punchy, entertaining, and convicting guide.

REBELS

RESCUED

BRIAN
COSBY

A STUDENTS
GUIDE TO
REFORMED
THEOLOGY

REBELS RESCUED

A Student's Guide to Reformed Theology
by Brian Cosby

ISBN: 978-1-84550-980-4

Have you ever had a shopping cart with a broken wheel? You push it around and all it wants to do is run into the sides of the aisle. If you were to let the cart go on its own, it would immediately turn and smash into that case of pickles up ahead! You are like that shopping cart! The bad wheel is your heart. It's always veering off, leading you away from what you were created to be.

You were created for God's love and glory, but instead, your heart pulls you away from Jesus and into something much worse than a case of pickles. Being a rebel at heart means that you do not have the ability to choose God or even to respond to God on your own, because you are spiritually dead; we all are. Reformed theology teaches that, because we are more sinful than we could ever imagine, it can only be God who takes that broken shopping cart wheel (our sinful heart) and replaces it with one that has both the ability and the desire to seek him and to follow him. By faith in Christ, you are no longer set to smash into the aisles of sinful destruction. No, he promises to carry us in his grip of grace.